Big Data Concepts, Technologies and Applications

With the advent of such advanced technologies as cloud computing, the Internet of Things, the Medical Internet of Things, the Industry Internet of Things and sensor networks as well as the exponential growth in the usage of Internet-based and social media platforms, there are enormous oceans of data. These huge volumes of data can be used for effective decision making and improved performance if analyzed properly. Due to its inherent characteristics, big data is very complex and cannot be handled and processed by traditional database management approaches. There is a need for sophisticated approaches, tools and technologies that can be used to store, manage and analyze these enormous amounts of data to make the best use of them.

Big Data Concepts, Technologies and Applications covers the concepts, technologies and applications of big data analytics. Presenting the state-of-the-art technologies in use for big data analytics, it provides an in-depth discussion about the important sectors where big data analytics has proven to be very effective in improving performance and helping industries to remain competitive. This book provides insight into the novel areas of big data analytics and the research directions for the scholars working in the domain. Highlights include:

- The advantages, disadvantages and challenges of big data analytics
- State-of-the-art technologies for big data analytics such as Hadoop, NoSQL databases, data lakes, deep learning and blockchain
- The application of big data analytics in healthcare, business, social media analytics, fraud detection and prevention and governance

Exploring the concepts and technologies behind big data analytics, the book is an ideal resource for researchers, students, data scientists, data analysts and business analysts who need insight into big data analytics.

Big Data Concepts, Technologies and Applications

Mohd. Shahid Husain,
Mohammad Zunnun Khan
and Tamanna Siddiqui

CRC Press
Taylor & Francis Group
Boca Raton London New York

CRC Press is an imprint of the
Taylor & Francis Group, an **informa** business

AN AUERBACH BOOK

First edition published 2024
by CRC Press
2385 Executive Center Drive, Suite 320, Boca Raton, FL 33431

and by CRC Press
4 Park Square, Milton Park, Abingdon, Oxon, OX14 4RN
CRC Press is an imprint of Taylor & Francis Group, LLC

© 2024 Taylor & Francis Group, LLC

ISBN: 9781032162751 (hbk)
ISBN: 9781032579184 (pbk)
ISBN: 9781003441595 (ebk)

DOI: 10.1201/9781003441595

Typeset in ITC Garamond Std
by Deanta Global Publishing Services, Chennai, India

Contents

Preface.. xiv

Acknowledgments xviii

List of Figures xx

List of Tables xxiii

About the Authors xxv

SECTION A   UNDERSTANDING BIG DATA

1   Overview of Big Data 3
    1.1   Introduction 3
    1.2   Types of Data 4
           1.2.1   Structured Data.. 4
           1.2.2   Unstructured Data 4
           1.2.3   Semi-Structured Data 5
    1.3   Evolution of Big Data 5
           1.3.1   Big Data Stage-1 5
           1.3.2   Big Data Stage-2 6
           1.3.3   Big Data Stage-3 7
    1.4   Big Data Characteristics 7
           1.4.1   Volume... 8
           1.4.2   Velocity 9
           1.4.3   Variety 9
           1.4.4   Veracity 9
           1.4.5   Value 10

1.5 Difference between Big Data and Data
Warehouse 10
1.6 Advantages and Disadvantages of Big Data............13
 1.6.1 Advantages..13
 1.6.2 Disadvantages of Big Data 13
1.7 Obstacles in Utilizing Big Data................................14
 1.7.1 Lack of Proper Understanding of Big Data 14
 1.7.2 Exponential Data Growth 15
 1.7.3 Confusion in Big Data Tool Selection...........16
 1.7.4 Securing Big Data..16
 1.7.5 Data Quality 17
 1.7.6 Lack of Expert Personnel 18
 1.7.7 Applications of Big Data 19
1.8 Impact of Big Data 21
References 21

2 Challenges of Big Data 22
2.1 Introduction 22
2.2 Big Data Integration 23
 2.2.1 Issues in Data Integration 23
 2.2.2 Approach to Data Integration 23
 2.2.3 Data Integration Methods..............................23
2.3 Storing Big Data 28
 2.3.1 Big Data Storage Methods.............................29
2.4 Maintaining Data Quality...30
 2.4.1 Data Quality Dimensions...............................31
 2.4.2 Data Quality Management Steps....................32
2.5 Analysis of Big Data...34
 2.5.1 Working Principle of Big Data Analytics......34
2.6 Security and Privacy Management............................36
 2.6.1 Need for Data Protection 36
 2.6.2 Challenges in Protecting Big Data 37
 2.6.3 Best Practices for Big Data Protection 37
2.7 Accessing and Sharing Information 39
References 39

3 Big Data Analytics **41**
   3.1   Introduction 41
   3.2   Applications of Big Data Analytics 42
         3.2.1   Traditional Business Applications of
               Big Data Analytics 42
         3.2.2   Recent Application Trends in
               Big Data Analytics 44
   3.3   Types of Big Data Analytics................................47
         3.3.1   Descriptive Analytics................................47
         3.3.2   Diagnostic Analytics................................49
         3.3.3   Predictive Analytics 50
         3.3.4   Prescriptive Analytics 52
   3.4   Comparison of Data Analytics Stages.....................54
   References 55

SECTION B   BIG DATA TECHNOLOGIES

4 Hadoop Ecosystem...**59**
   4.1   Introduction 59
   4.2   Components of the Hadoop Ecosystem...................60
         4.2.1   Data Storage...60
         4.2.2   Data Processing 61
         4.2.3   Data Access..61
         4.2.4   Data Management.....................................61
   4.3   Data Storage Component 62
         4.3.1   Google File System (GFS)...........................62
         4.3.2   Hadoop Distributed File System (HDFS) 62
         4.3.3   HBase...65
   4.4   Data Processing Component................................. 68
         4.4.1   MapReduce 68
         4.4.2   YARN 69
   4.5   Data Access Component 71
         4.5.1   Hive...71
         4.5.2   Apache Pig...72
         4.5.3   Apache Drill..73

4.5.4   Apache Sqoop...73

4.5.5   Apache Avro 74

4.5.6   Apache Mahout...75

4.6   Data Management Component 75

4.6.1   ZooKeeper 75

4.6.2   Oozie.. 77

4.6.3   Ambari 77

4.6.4   Apache Flume 78

4.7   Apache Spark..79

References 79

5   **NoSQL Databases 81**

5.1   Introduction 81

5.1.1   Features of NoSQL.......................................81

5.1.2   Difference between NoSQL and SQL 83

5.2   Types of NoSQL Databases....................................83

5.2.1 Types of NoSQL Databases 85

5.3   Key-Value Pair Based Storage 85

5.4   Column-Oriented Databases.................................. 86

5.5   Document-Oriented Databases...............................87

5.6   Graph-Based Databases 88

5.7   Summary of NoSQL Databases..............................89

5.8   BASE Model of NoSQL...89

5.8.1   CAP Theorem 91

5.8.2   BASE Model 92

5.8.3   ACID vs BASE Model 93

5.9   Advantages of NoSQL 93

5.10 Disadvantages of NoSQL..94

References 95

6   **Data Lakes 96**

6.1   Introduction 96

6.2   Data Lake Architecture...97

6.2.1   Transient Zone..97

6.2.2   Raw Zone.. 98

6.2.3   Trusted Zone 98

6.2.4   Refined Zone 98

6.3   Usage of Data Lakes.. 98
       6.3.1   Facilitating Data Science and Machine
                Learning Capabilities 99
       6.3.2   Centralizing, Consolidating and
                Cataloguing Data 99
       6.3.3   Seamless Integration of Diverse Data
                Sources and Formats 100
       6.3.4   Offering Various Self-Service Tools.............100
6.4   Data Lake Challenges..100
       6.4.1   Data Swamps 100
       6.4.2   Slow Performance..100
       6.4.3   Lack of Security Features 101
       6.4.4   Reliability Issues 101
6.5   Data Lake Advantages and Disadvantages............101
6.6   Lake House..101
       6.6.1   Delta Lake 103
6.7   Difference between Data Warehouses, Data
       Lakes and Lake Houses..103
6.8   Best Practices Regarding Data Lakes.....................105
       6.8.1   Data Lake as Landing Zone 105
       6.8.2   Data Quality 105
       6.8.3   Reliability 105
       6.8.4   Data Catalog 105
       6.8.5   Security 106
       6.8.6   Privacy 106
       6.8.7   Data Lineage..106
References 106

7 **Deep Learning 108**
7.1   Introduction..108
7.2   Deep Learning Architecture...................................109
       7.2.1   Supervised Learning....................................110
       7.2.2   Unsupervised Learning 114
7.3   Training Approaches for Deep Learning Models.......117
       7.3.1   Training from Scratch.................................117
       7.3.2   Transfer Learning..118
       7.3.3   Feature Extraction 118

7.4 Challenges in Deep Learning Implementation....... 119
 7.4.1 Data Volume Required 119
 7.4.2 Biasness... 119
 7.4.3 Explainability 119
7.5 Applications of Deep Learning............................120
 7.5.1 Healthcare Industry.................................120
 7.5.2 Autonomous Vehicles 120
 7.5.3 E-Commerce 120
 7.5.4 Personal Assistant.....................................121
 7.5.5 Medical Research 121
 7.5.6 Customer Service 121
 7.5.7 Finance Industry.......................................121
 7.5.8 Industrial Automation..............................122
 7.5.9 Smart Devices..122
 7.5.10 Aerospace and Defense............................122
 7.5.11 Weather Predictions..................................122
References 122

8 Blockchain 124
8.1 Introduction 124
8.2 Structure of the Blockchain 124
8.3 Security Features of the Blockchain 126
 8.3.1 Block Linking 126
 8.3.2 Consensus Mechanism 126
8.4 Types of Blockchain...126
 8.4.1 Public Blockchain......................................126
 8.4.2 Private Blockchain.....................................127
 8.4.3 Consortium Blockchain.............................128
 8.4.4 Hybrid Blockchain.....................................128
8.5 Blockchain Evolution...129
 8.5.1 The First Generation (Blockchain 1.0:
    Cryptocurrency)...130
 8.5.2 The Second Generation (Blockchain 2.0:
    Smart Contracts) 130
 8.5.3 The Third Generation (Blockchain 3.0:
    DApps) 132
 8.5.4 The Fourth Generation (Blockchain 4.0:
    Industry Applications) 132

8.6   Advantages of Blockchain 132
8.7   Disadvantages of Blockchain 133
        8.7.1   Security Risk 134
        8.7.2   Speed and Performance 134
        8.7.3   Scalability..134
        8.7.4   Data Modification 134
        8.7.5   High Implementation Cost 134
8.8   Applications of Blockchain 135
        8.8.1   Banking and Financial Industry.................135
        8.8.2   Healthcare industry 135
        8.8.3   Supply Chain Management 135
        8.8.4   Food Chain Management............................136
        8.8.5   Governance...136
        8.8.6   Internet of Things Network Management....136
References 136

SECTION C   BIG DATA APPLICATIONS

9   Big Data for Healthcare 139
9.1   Introduction 139
9.2   Benefits of Big Data Analytics in Healthcare 139
        9.2.1   Improved Healthcare.................................140
        9.2.2   Pervasive Healthcare 141
        9.2.3   Drug Discovery..142
        9.2.4   Reduced Cost..142
        9.2.5   Risk Prediction...142
        9.2.6   Early Detection of the Spread of
                  Diseases...142
        9.2.7   Fraud Detection and Prevention 142
        9.2.8   Clinical Operations.....................................143
9.3   Challenges in Implementing Big Data in
        Healthcare..143
        9.3.1   Confidentiality and Data Security...............143
        9.3.2   Data Aggregation..144
        9.3.3   Reliability 144
        9.3.4   Access Control 144
        9.3.5   Interoperability 145
References 145

10 Big Data Analytics for Fraud Detection..............148

10.1 Introduction...148

10.2 Types of Fraud...149

    10.2.1 Insurance Fraud...150

    10.2.2 Network Intrusion 150

    10.2.3 Credit Card Fraud 150

    10.2.4 Money Laundering..150

    10.2.5 Accounting Fraud..151

    10.2.6 Financial Markets Fraud 151

    10.2.7 Telecommunication Fraud 151

10.3 Fraud Detection and Prevention 152

    10.3.1 Traditional Fraud Detection Methods 152

    10.3.2 Big Data Analytics for Fraud Detection......154

10.4 Features Used for Fraud Detection 155

10.5 Benefits of Big Data Analytics for
Fraud Detection..156

10.6 Applications of Big Data Analytics for Fraud
Detection 157

10.7 Issues in Implementing Big Data Analytics for
Fraud Detection...157

References 159

11 Big Data Analytics in Social Media 161

11.1 Introduction...161

11.2 Types of Social Media Platforms............................162

11.3 Social Media Statistics 163

11.4 Big Data Analytics in Social Media 164

    11.4.1 Analytic Techniques 164

11.5 Applications of Big Data Analytics in
Social Media 168

    11.5.1 Business 170

    11.5.2 Disaster Management 170

    11.5.3 Healthcare...171

    11.5.4 Governance..171

11.6 Key Challenges in Social Media Analytics 172

References 173

**12 Novel Applications and Research
Directions in Big Data Analytics 175**

12.1   Introduction 175

12.2   Education Sector 175

12.3   Agriculture Sector 176

12.4   Entertainment Industry 177

12.5   Manufacturing 178

12.6   Renewable Energy 179

12.7   Business Applications 179

12.8   Financial Services 180

12.9   Sport 181

12.10 Politics 181

References 182

Index 185

Preface

Big data is a buzz world in recent times. Big data is defined on the basis of multiple factors. The common Vs used to define big data characteristics are velocity, volume, variety, variability and veracity.

Velocity represents the enormous speed with which the data is generated. **Volume** represents the amount of data generated that needs to be processed. **Variety** reflects that this huge volume of data is generated from multiple sources of a heterogeneous nature, namely structured, semi-structured and unstructured forms of data. Variety also represents that this data is in different forms like text, audio, video and signals. **Variability** reflects that this data keeps changing/updating. **Veracity** defines one of the key characteristics of big data, that there is a need to verify the authenticity of every data item before using it for analysis.

Big data analytics enables large volumes of data to be acquired from multiple heterogeneous sources, preprocessing it to make it application-ready, maintaining large-scale data storage and applying sophisticated machine learning techniques to get insights useful for targeted applications.

Emerging Need

With the advent of advanced technologies like cloud computing, the Internet of Things, Medical Internet of Things, Industry

Internet of Things, sensor networks and the exponential growth in the usage of the Internet and social media platforms, we have an enormous ocean of data. These huge volumes of data can be used for effective decision making and improved performance if analyzed properly. Due to its inherent characteristics, big data is very complex and cannot be handled and processed by traditional database management approaches. There is a need for sophisticated approaches, tools and technologies which can be used to store, manage and analyze this enormous amount of data to make the best use of it.

Purpose

This book will provide in-depth knowledge about the concepts, technologies and application areas of big data analytics. The book will deal with the state-of-the-art technologies in use for big data analytics. It will provide in-depth discussion about the important sectors where big data analytics has proved to be very effective in improving performance and is helping industries to remain competitive. This book will give insight into the novel areas of big data analytics and the research directions for the scholars working in the domain.

Audience

This book will explore the concepts and technologies behind big data analytics. Technologies like Hadoop, NoSQL databases, data lakes, deep learning and blockchain are the current demands of the market. The book will assist individuals as well as organizations in understanding and implementing big data analytics in their systems. It will be an ideal resource for researchers, students, data scientists, data analysts and business analysts to get insight into the state of the art in big data analytics.

Emphasis

This book deals with various aspects of the successful implementation of big data analytics using the latest technologies along with the challenges in big data analytics implementation. It also provides insights into how big data analytics is impacting various industries and what the future of big data analytics will be.

What You Will Learn

By going through the material presented in this book, you will learn:

- The concept of big data analytics, why it is needed and how it can contribute to improving performance for different sectors or industries.
- The advantages, disadvantages and challenges of big data analytics.
- Applications of big data analytics in various sectors.
- State-of-the-art technologies for big data analytics.
- The latest trends in big data analytics.
- The use of big data analytics approaches for different applications like healthcare, business, social media analytics, fraud detection and prevention, governance and many more.

Book Organization

The book is divided into three sections. Section A (Chapters 1–3) of the book provides the conceptual background, starting with an overview of big data and big data analytics, the challenges of big data analytics andbig data analytics techniques. This is followed by Section B (Chapters 5–8). This section discusses state-of-the-art technologies, like Hadoop, deep learning and blockchain, used for big data analytics. The final part of the book, Section C (Chapters 9–12), deals with different applications of big data analytics and future research directions.

Acknowledgments

This work was a great experience for us in the domain of big data analytics. There are lots of people who helped us, directly and indirectly, to make this book a reality. We would like to acknowledge the contribution of each individual who helped us in the conception and completion of this book.

We want to take this opportunity to offer our sincere gratitude to them. A very special thanks to the CRC publication team, particularly Stephanie Kiefer and John Wyzalek, without their continuous encouragement and support this book would not have been possible. We also thank esteemed technical experts Dr. T J Siddiqui (Prof., University of Allahabad), Dr. Rashid Ali (Prof. AMU Aligarh), Adil Kaleem (Cloud Delivery Technical Architect at NCS Group, Australia), Dr. Mohammad Suaib (Assoc. Prof., Integral University) and Dr. M Akbar (Assoc. Prof., Integral University) for their efforts in time-constrained impartial and critical reviews, proofreading and providing constructive feedback.

Thanks to our friends and colleagues for providing help wherever and whenever necessary.

This acknowledgment will not be complete until we share our gratitude and pay our regards to our parents and family members for their unflinching encouragement to us in all of our pursuits. It's the confidence of our family members in us that has made us the people that we are today. We dedicate this book to them.

Finally, we wish to thank the organizations and individuals who granted us permission to use the research material and information necessary for the completion of this book.

Last but not least, we are heartily thankful to almighty God for showering His blessings forever during our entire lives.

List of Figures

Figure 1.1 Evolution stages of big data. 5

Figure 1.2 Big data characteristics. 8

Figure 1.3 Data quality parameters. 17

Figure 1.4 Application area of big data analytics. 19

Figure 1.5 Impact of big data analytics. 20

Figure 2.1 Link-driven federation data integration
architecture. 24

Figure 2.2 Data warehousing architecture. 25

Figure 2.3 Mediation architecture for data integration. 26

Figure 2.4 Big data integration stages. 27

Figure 2.5 Big data quality dimensions. 31

Figure 3.1 Traditional business applications of
big data analytics. 42

Figure 3.2 Latest trends in big data analytics. 45

Figure 3.3 Types of big data analytics. 48

Figure 4.1 Layers in Hadoop Ecosystem. 61

Figure 4.2 HDFS architecture. 63

Figure 4.3 MapReduce architecture. 69

Figure 4.4   YARN architecture.................................70

Figure 5.1   Example of documented-oriented database...... 88

Figure 5.2   Graph-oriented data store................................89

Figure 5.3   ACID vs BASE model. 93

Figure 6.1   Data lake architecture with zones. 98

Figure 7.1   Deep learning architectures 110

Figure 7.2   Convolutional neural network architecture...... 111

Figure 7.3a   LSTM architecture.................................112

Figure 7.3b   GRU architecture.................................112

Figure 7.4   SOM architecture (with two clusters
and n input features).. 114

Figure 7.5   Autoencoder architecture. 115

Figure 7.6   Restricted Boltzmann machine architecture..... 116

Figure 7.7   Deep belief network architecture. 117

Figure 7.8   Training approaches for deep learning
models..118

Figure 8.1   Structure of a block..125

Figure 8.2   Structure of blockchain......................................125

Figure 8.3   Types of blockchain..127

Figure 8.4   Evolution of blockchain. 130

Figure 9.1   Key sources of healthcare big data...................140

Figure 9.2   Benefits of big data analytics in healthcare. 141

Figure 9.3   Challenges of big data analytics
in healthcare 143

Figure 10.1   Types of fraud. 149

Figure 10.2   Fraud detection methods. 153

Figure 11.1 Data generation through social media platforms 162

Figure 11.2 Types of social media platforms 162

Figure 11.3 Active users (in billions) on social media 163

Figure 11.4 Reason for social media usage 164

Figure 11.5 Social media analytic approaches. 166

Figure 11.6 Usage of social media analytic approaches 166

Figure 11.7 Impact of social media analytics. 169

List of Tables

Table 1.1 Evolution of Big Data 6

Table 1.2 Comparison of Data Warehouse and Big Data 11

Table 2.1 Big Data Intrinsic and Contextual Quality Dimensions 32

Table 3.1 Comparison of Data Analytics Stages...................54

Table 4.1 Comparison between Traditional System and Hadoop Ecosystem...60

Table 4.2 GFS vs HDFS...66

Table 4.3 Bigtable vs HBase 67

Table 4.4 HDFS vs HBase 68

Table 5.1 Differences between SQL and NoSQL.................84

Table 5.2 Example of Key-Value Store....................................85

Table 5.3 Column-Oriented Database Structure 86

Table 5.4 Example of Column-Oriented Database..............87

Table 5.5 Summary of Different Types of NoSQL Databases 90

Table 5.6 Comparison of ACID Model and BASE Model.........94

Table 6.1 Advantages and Disadvantages of Data Lakes........102

Table 6.2 Differences between Data Warehouses, Data Lakes and Lake Houses 104

Table 8.1 Types of Blockchains 129

Table 8.2 Comparison of Blockchain Generations 131

Table 10.1 Features for Fraud Detection............................156

About the Authors

Dr. Mohd. Shahid Husain is a research professional and faculty member with 14 years of teaching and research experience. He is currently working as assistant professor in the College of Computing and Information Sciences – Ibri, University of Technology and Applied Sciences, Oman.

He obtained his M.Tech. in information technology (spl: intelligent systems) from the Indian Institute of Information Technology, Allahabad (www.iiita.ac.in), India. He received his Ph.D. in computer science and engineering from Integral University, Lucknow (www.iul.ac.in), India. His areas of interest include artificial intelligence, information retrieval, natural language processing, data mining, web mining, data analytics, sentiment analysis and computer networks and security. Dr. Mohd. Shahid Husain has published 6 books, 14 book chapters and more than 30 research papers in journals/conferences of international repute. He has been involved with many sponsored projects as PI/Co-PI. Currently, he is working on two funded projects submitted to the Research Council (TRC), Oman. He also contributes his knowledge and experience as a guest speaker, doctorial committee member, session chair, member of the editorial board/advisory committee and Technical Program Committee member in various international journals/conferences of repute. Dr. Mohd Shahid Husain is an active member of different professional bodies including IEEE Young Professionals, IEEE-TCII, ISTE, CSTA and IACSIT.

Dr. Mohd Shahid Husain passed the UGC National Eligibility Test (NET) in June 2014 and the Graduate Aptitude Test in Engineering (GATE) in 2008.

He obtained two specialization certificates in Python and applied data science from the University of Michigan in 2020.

mohammad.shahid@utas.edu.om; siddiquisahil@gmail.com

Dr. Mohammad Zunnun Khan works as assistant professor in the College of Computing and Information Technology, the University of Bisha, Kingdom of Saudi Arabia. He has more than ten years of research and academic experience.

He earned his Bachelor's, Master's and Ph.D. degrees in the field of computer science and engineering. He has authored around 20 research articles on different topics related to computer science and engineering, in various national and international journals and conferences of repute. He has also contributed as an editorial board and reviewer board member of different international and national conferences and journals. His areas of interest include data science, cloud quality, security, software quality and security and data mining. He has also published one book and authored around five book chapters. Dr. Mohammad Zunnun Khan is also a member of myriad professional bodies including CSI and IEEE.

zunnunkhan@gmail.com

Prof. Tamanna Siddiqui is presently working as professor in the Department of Computer Science, Aligarh Muslim University (AMU), Aligarh (UP), India. She also worked as Training and Placement Officer in the Department of Computer Science, AMU, Aligarh (UP) from 2014 to 2021. She obtained her B.Sc. (Maths) Hons. and MCA from AMU, Aligarh, and her Ph.D. incomputer science from Jamia Hamdard, New Delhi. She has 23 years of rich teaching experience at the national and international level, which includes 12 years in Jamia Hamdard, New Delhi, 3 years in the University of Dammam, KSA, and 8 years in AMU, Aligarh (UP). She contributed to the revision of the bylaws and curriculum of both universities. She contributed to various administrative works at Jamia Hamdard such as deputy superintendent examinations, officiating head, MCA course coordinator, warden, etc. She worked as a member of the recruitment committee of the College of Computer Science and Information Technology, University of Dammam, KSA, for a period of three years. She has been acknowledged by Wasit University Iraq and the University of Dammam for her excellence in teaching and research. She has a large number of publications in reputed international/national journals/conferences, like the *Journal of Advances in Information Technology* (Academy Publisher), *International Journal on Computer Science and Engineering* (IJCSE), *International Journal of Information Technology, International Journal of Advanced Computer Science and Applications* (IJACSA) (IEEE Xplore, Springer), *Communications in Computer and Information Science,* LNCS, etc. She is a member of the Indian Society of Technical Education, the International Association of Computer Science and Information Technology, the Engineering and Scientific Research Group, etc. She was a member of the Academic

Council, Board of Research Studies (BRS) and Board of Studies (BOS) in Jamia Hamdard. She has also contributed as editor, member of the advisory board, reviewer, program committee member, keynote speaker, etc., to many international journals and conferences. Her research interests include data mining, databases, software engineering, cloud applications, big data analytics, etc. Presently six students are pursuing Ph.D. degrees and seven students have been awarded Ph.D. degrees under her supervision.

tsiddiqui.cs@amu.ac.in; ja_zu_siddiqui@hotmail.com

UNDERSTANDING A
BIG DATA

Chapter 1

Overview of Big Data

1.1 Introduction

Big data is a term that refers to data that is both extremely large in volume and consists of complex datasets. With the advent of new technologies, the data on the World Wide Web has increased explosively in the past few decades. The ability to automatically extract useful information from this massive amount of data has been a common concern for organizations (Khan, 2015).

The term "big data" was first coined by John R Mashey in the 1990s, and since then it has gained in popularity and become a buzz word. However, the concept of using a huge volume of data repositories to extract useful information is not something new. Around 300 BC, the library of Alexandria in ancient Egypt had a huge repository of data from almost every domain. Similarly, big civilizations and empires like the Roman Empire and the Ottoman Empire had well-maintained records of all kinds of resources which were carefully analyzed for decision making and the optimal distribution of resources across different regions.

However, it has certainly evolved over a long period of time. During the last few decades, the generation of

DOI: 10.1201/9781003441595-2

data has exponentially increased in terms of volume and speed. According to a report by Statista (Statista Research Department, 2022), the amount of total data created, captured, copied and consumed globally in 2022 was approximately 97 zettabytes with projected growth of around 180 zettabytes by the year 2025. We can make use of this enormous amount of data available for decision making and get more accurate and updated information, but traditional data analysis methods can't cope with this big data. For the effective analysis and use of this huge volume of data we need sophisticated tools and techniques.

1.2 Types of Data

Data generated across the variety of applications can be divided into the following three broad categories.

1.2.1 Structured Data

Data content which follows a specific format or structure is referred to as structured data. For most organizations, the data generated through Online Transaction Processing (OLTP) systems is structured data because it follows a particular format. This structured data is machine readable and can be saved, accessed and processed using traditional approaches like structured query languages (SQL) to extract information for user queries. Around 20% of the data in the world is structured data. The data in relational database tables and spreadsheets are the most common examples of structured data.

1.2.2 Unstructured Data

Data content which doesn't follow any specific predefined format is called unstructured data. "Unstructured data" refers to a heterogeneous data source that includes a variety of data in addition to plain text files, such as images, videos, signal data and other media. This unstructured data is not machine readable, and hence processing unstructured data is quite a complex job as traditional techniques (following structured format) are not effective. Currently most of the data generated using web, mobile devises, sensor networks, etc., is unstructured, and we need sophisticated techniques to handle it.

1.2.3 Semi-Structured Data

Data content which is not fully structured but follows some degree of organization in its presentation is called semi-structured data. We need to preprocess this data to make it machine readable. Most of the web content developed using HTML and XML is semi-structured data.

1.3 Evolution of Big Data

Big data can be better understood by looking at how it evolved from traditional data analysis in multiple stages over a period of time. As shown in Figure 1.1, there are three stages in the evolution of big data which are summarized in Table 1.1.

1.3.1 Big Data Stage-1

Traditionally, data is stored, processed and extracted using a database management system like relational database management systems (RDBS). Later on, organizations have started to archive historical data using data warehouses. Techniques

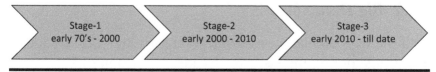

Figure 1.1   Evolution stages of big data.

Table 1.1   Evolution of Big Data

Evolution Stage	Duration	Features
Stage-1	From the early 1970s to 2000	Traditional database management systems based on structured content like RDBMS and data warehouses. Targeted applications are: OLTP- and OLAP-based processing Use of typical data mining techniques
Stage-2	From early 2000 to 2010	Focus shifted to extracting information from web-based unstructured content. Targeted applications are: Information retrieval (IR) systems Sentiment analysis or opinion mining Social media analytics Question answering systems
Stage-3	From early 2010 to date	The storing and manipulation of sensor data generated from mainly mobile devices and other sensor networks. Targeted applications are: Spatial-temporal analysis Emotion analysis and subjective satisfaction IoT, MIoT, IIoT, etc.

like database queries, reporting tools, Online Transaction Processing (OLTP) and Online Analytical Processing (OLAP) are the core concepts of modern-day data analytics and big data. During this period mainly structured data is used for analysis and decision-making purposes.

1.3.2 Big Data Stage-2

With the exponential growth of the Internet and World Wide Web usage during the last two decades, companies like Yahoo, Amazon and eBay have found a new way to better understand their customers and users by analyzing totally different kinds of data like IP addresses, browsing history, click-rates and search logs. The surge in HTTP-based web traffic has resulted in a considerable increase in semi-structured and unstructured data in addition to the normal structured data. Businesses have had to create more sophisticated ways to analyze and extract information from these sources which are comprised of a variety of data. With the advent of social media and other web-based platforms for sharing data, the need for the latest and most effective tools, systems and approaches for extracting useful information from unstructured data has grown.

1.3.3 Big Data Stage-3

In spite of the fact that many organizations' major focus is still web-based unstructured content for data analytics, mobile devices are now emerging as the prime source for the acquisition of vital information. For example, mobile devices enable the storage and analysis of temporal-spatial data in addition to the user's behavioral data based on their web navigation patterns.

The latest trends based on sensor technologies like the Internet of things (IoT), industrial Internet of things (IIoT), medical Internet of things (MIoT), body sensor networks (BSN), etc., are generating huge volumes of data with a speed which has never been seen before.

1.4 Big Data Characteristics

Big data is normally described in terms of V's. Initially the most popular three V's were volume, velocity and variety (Khan, 2017). However, in some sources one can find up to 40 V's used to define big data. The five most relevant V's (other V's are derived from these five) are shown in Figure 1.2.

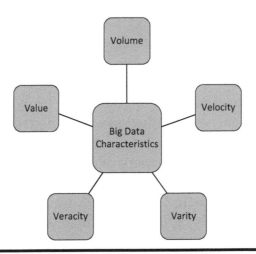

Figure 1.2 Big data characteristics.

1.4.1 Volume

A significant quantity of data is referred to as a "volume." One of the key characteristics of big data is its huge volume. The quantity of the data is an important factor to consider when using it for analysis. The term "big data" refers to situations in which the quantity of data to be processed is extraordinarily large. Hence, the quantity of data is the critical factor in determining whether or not a collection of data can be referred to as big data. As a consequence of this, it is absolutely necessary to take into consideration a certain "volume" when working with big data.

1.4.1.1 Fact

There are approximately 44 zettabytes of data in the world in 2020. Based on the amount of data generated every day it will likely be 175 zettabytes by 2025 (Vuleta, 2021). Approximately 2.5 quintillion bytes of data is generated every day (Prodanoff, 2022), and this is expected to reach 463 exabytes per day by 2025 (Bulao, 2022).

1.4.2 Velocity

The term "velocity" refers to the rate of the data generation or how fast the data is generated as well as processed. Currently data is generated at a high speed from sensor networks, high processing computing machines, social media, the digital entertainment industry, mobile phones and other sources. This content generated with high velocity represents big data. As new data is coming at a very high speed, for effective information capturing we need methods for real time data analysis.

1.4.2.1 Fact

Approximately 18.7 billion text messages are created every day. Facebook generates around four petabytes of data every day (Vuleta, 2021).

1.4.3 Variety

Variety refers to the different forms of data, i.e. whether the data is structured, unstructured or semi-structured. Additionally, it also refers to a multitude of different data sources. IBM estimates that over 90% of real time data is unstructured data. In most cases, it is used to refer to data that does not neatly fit into the traditional row and column structure of a relational database. Text, images and videos are examples of types of data that cannot be organized into rows and columns and are therefore considered to be unstructured.

1.4.4 Veracity

Veracity refers to the reliability of data to be used for analysis purposes. It's a challenging task in the case of big data to maintain the data's high quality and precision due to the inherent variability and unpredictability of data sources. Big data is prone to unpredictability because it contains a large number of data dimensions that are derived from a large number of different data types and sources. It is hard to validate the authenticity and accuracy of the data collected from such sources.

1.4.5 Value

For any organization, all data available does not have the same usability or value. The raw data does not have any value or significance on its own; in order to derive useful information from it, it must first be preprocessed and transformed as per the needs of the organization. In the ocean of big data one may get lost and make wrong decisions if the data is acquired from irrelevant or unreliable sources. Identifying the relevant sources and valuable content based on the organizational requirements from this high volume of data is one of the most important factors.

1.5 Difference between Big Data and Data Warehouse

Big data refers to extremely huge volumes of data generated with rapid speed from multiple sources. The conventional tools and databases for processing data are unable to handle this enormous volume of data, which may be structured, semi-structured or unstructured. Before being used by businesses to make decisions that are in line with their best interests, data goes through a number of processes, including analysis and modifications.

In the context of the modern business world, large amounts of data are an extremely valuable asset. Big data may also be used to solve problems in corporations by enabling more informed decision making, which is one of the benefits of using big data.

A **data warehouse** is a repository of data acquired from multiple sources. A data warehouse stores day to day transactional data as well, but the key component of a data warehouse is the historical data of past years. It is the most important part of a business intelligence system and serves as the hub for the collection, organization and evaluation of archival data with the purpose of enhancing decision making. The extraction, loading and processing of the data are required in order to make it available for analysis. Large-scale data queries can be performed with the help of data warehouses which provide a different perspective for decision making at different levels. It aids in the creation of analytical reports by means of data extraction from a number of SQL-based data sources (primarily relational databases).

Prominent dissimilarities in big data and data warehouses are summarized in Table 1.2.

Table 1.2   Comparison of Data Warehouse and Big Data

Comparison Criteria	Big Data	Data Warehouse
Conceptual definition	Big data is defined in terms of its volume, the amount of data coming from various sources, its velocity and the number of distinct sorts of data (mainly support all types of data format). It is a technology that is notable for its capacity to store and manage massive amounts of data.	The term "data warehouse" is more accurately applied to a structure than a specific type of technology. The data warehouse refers to a centralized data repository from which multiple analytical report types can be generated. It is a framework for organizing the data that is being used.

(Continued)

Table 1.2 Continued

Comparison Criteria	Big Data	Data Warehouse
Business application	Companies favor the big data methodology if they need to analyze massive amounts of data in order to make informed business decisions such as how to increase sales, profits and client base size.	Data warehousing is the preferred option when a company needs a credible report (such as an overview of what's happening within the company, projections for the coming year based on past performance, etc.) to make an informed decision.
Data sources	Data can be acquired from any source, be it a traditional commercial transaction, a social media post or raw data collected by a sensor or machine. It need not be a DBMS-related product at all.	Data is integrated from a variety of sources, both homogeneous and heterogeneous (using the same or different DBMS products at each site).
Data types and formats	Data can be in any form like text files, emails, videos, audio files, sensor data and financial transactions which can be structured, semi-structured or unstructured.	Works primarily with structured data (specifically relational data).
Query	Big data doesn't have any structured query language to retrieve the information needed.	A data warehouse uses structured query language to respond to users' information needs.

1.6 Advantages and Disadvantages of Big Data

Big data provides a lot of benefits by making use of the vast volume of data available to get valuable information and make better decisions. However, there are some key points which make the handling of big data disadvantageous for organizations.

1.6.1 Advantages

Some of the key benefits of big data are:

- It provides better business insight.
- It helps in developing innovative solutions.
- It helps in understanding and targeting customers.
- It helps in improving customer service.
- It helps in increased productivity.
- It helps in fraud detection.
- It helps in increased agility.
- It helps in better decision making.
- It helps in cost optimization.
- It helps in optimizing business processes.
- It helps in improving science and research.
- It improves healthcare systems.
- It helps in financial trading.
- It helps in security and law enforcement.

1.6.2 Disadvantages of Big Data

The main concerns in handling big data are:

- It costs a lot of money to store and maintain big data.
- Most big data content is unstructured.
- Big data analysis may risk individuals' privacy.
- It is hard to maintain compliance with legal issues.
- Data can be manipulated with the wrong intentions.
- It may increase social stratification.
- In many cases big data analytics can give you incorrect results.

- Due to real time data generation, big data can fail to match real figures.
- There is a lack of skilled persons to perform big data analytics.
- There are security risks like authentication, reliability, trust, etc.

1.7 Obstacles in Utilizing Big Data

The problems of big data are complex to analyze and solve. It's common for companies to become bogged down in the early phases of implementing big data projects. One way to avoid this is to classify the problem according to the data format. Using big data effectively requires a shift in how businesses operate. For the effective utilization of big data, organizations need to improve the quality of the workforce and change management and look at present business practices and technologies. With the guidance of a chief data officer, several Fortune 500 companies have been able to make better business decisions. It is really very difficult to handle big data in every field. These challenges include the requirement of high computation and storage power, the design of new advanced architecture, sophisticated algorithms, visualization techniques, etc. The main challenges in handling big data are:

1.7.1 Lack of Proper Understanding of Big Data

Companies' attempts to exploit big data often end in failure due to a lack of knowledge on the subject. It's possible that employees don't know what data is needed or how it should be stored, processed and sourced. When employees don't realize how crucial data storage is, they may not keep a backup of critical information. It's possible that they aren't properly storing data in their databases. Thus, it is difficult to locate this crucial data when it is needed.

1.7.1.1 Solution

Big data workshops and seminars should be offered to all employees at their workplaces. Training should be given to all employees that handle data on a regular basis and are participating in big data projects, regardless of their position. Data concepts must be understood at all levels of the organization.

1.7.2 Exponential Data Growth

A major worry with big data is how to safely store the enormous amount of data that will be generated. The amount of information stored in data centers and corporate databases is increasing at a rapid pace. As the volume of data grows, it becomes increasingly difficult to handle it.

Documents, videos, audio files and other media make up the vast majority of big data which can't be stored and processed using traditional approaches.

1.7.2.1 Solution

Current techniques like compression and deduplication are being used to deal with these enormous datasets. As a result of data compression, the overall size of a file is reduced. Deduplication is the process of removing redundant data from a dataset.

Data tiering allows companies to store data in separate storage tiers. As a result, the data is stored in the best possible place. Data tiers might include public clouds, private clouds and flash storage, depending on their size and importance.

Dimensionality reduction is another approach used to manage high volumes of data.

Big data technologies such as Hadoop, NoSQL and others are also being adopted by businesses.

1.7.3 Confusion in Big Data Tool Selection

Companies are often confused when it comes to choosing the best tool for big data analysis and storage for their purpose. Questions like whether they should go for HBase or Cassandra to store data, or whether Spark will outperform Hadoop MapReduce in terms of data analytics and storage trouble companies, and they are usually unable to find solutions to these queries. Due to these confusions they may make bad decisions and end up opting for ineffective technologies/tools for their purpose. Picking the wrong tools for big data storage and analysis leads to the wasting of critical resources, such as time, money, effort and work hours.

1.7.3.1 Solution

Getting help from an expert is always the best option. Alternatively, you can hire seasoned professionals who have a more in-depth understanding of these instruments. Big data consultants can also be hired who can help you in selecting the best tools for your company's needs.

1.7.4 Securing Big Data

One of the most challenging aspects of big data is securing this massive volume of data. Most of the time organizations utilize all of their resources in better understanding, maintaining and analyzing the data acquired, and they ignore the security aspect (Mohammad Shahid Husain, 2019). Unsecured data repositories can be easily exploited by malicious hackers and lead to huge losses for companies.

1.7.4.1 Solution

To secure data repositories and protect data some measures are:

■ Encrypt data for storage and transmission
■ Segregate data in different categories

- Authenticate using identity verification
- Enable access control mechanisms for authorization
- Use log files
- Real time security monitoring
- Employ cyber security experts
- Use big data security software tools

1.7.5 Data Quality

Quality of data is a major concern in getting valuable information to satisfy the user's needs. Bad data leads to inaccurate information and bad decision making. Key parameters to assess the quality of data are shown in Figure 1.3.

Figure 1.3 Data quality parameters.

High-quality data ensures that the data is adequate to serve the specific needs of an organization in a particular context. Factors that negatively affect data quality are:

■ Inconsistency
■ Incompleteness
■ Redundancy
■ Unorganized data
■ Ambiguous and ill-defined data

As data volumes increase exponentially, methods to improve and ensure big data quality are critical in making accurate, effective and trusted business decisions.

1.7.5.1 Solution

Organizations should formalize standard data quality rules by which all data across the organization should be governed. These standards should be used to integrate data from various internal and external sources, create and monitor data usage policies, eliminate inconsistencies and inaccuracies and implement regulatory compliance.

Acquired data should be interpreted and assessed by experts based on quality parameters, and low-quality data should be avoided in analysis because it can lead to poor decision making.

1.7.6 Lack of Expert Personnel

With the advent of new technologies and the provision of effective big data solutions there is a need for trained data specialists. The industry lacks expert professionals like data scientists, analysts and engineers who have good experience in using the tools and analyzing large datasets. Most professionals haven't kept pace with the rapid advancements in data processing tools. To close the gap, concrete actions must be taken.

1.7.6.1 Solution

Organizations are spending more time and money in search of top-notch experts. In order to get the most out of their current personnel they must provide training for the required big data skills. In this way they can reduce the recruitment costs significantly. AI/ML-powered data analytics solutions can be purchased by small-scale corporations which can be utilized by people who aren't expert professionals but have some knowledge of data analytics.

1.7.7 Applications of Big Data

Big data analytics has proven its utility in almost every sector as shown in Figure 1.4. In order to realize their full potential and engage in effective strategy planning industries are gradually turning toward big data utilization.

Here is the list of the top 20 industries using big data applications:

- Financial and banking sector
- Insurance sector
- Communications, media and entertainment
- Healthcare
- Education

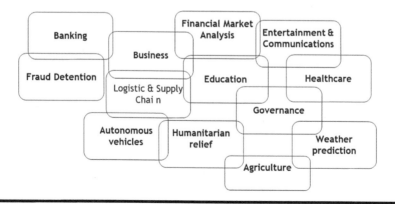

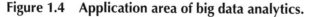

Figure 1.4   Application area of big data analytics.

- E-governance
- E-commerce
- Marketing
- Retail and wholesale trade
- Transportation
- Manufacturing and natural resources
- Energy and utilities
- Social media
- IoT
- Tourism industry
- Scientific research
- Pharmaceutical industry
- Cyber security
- Fraud detection
- Agriculture

Social and Ethical
- Improved awareness
- Improved efficiency
- Participation
- Trust
- Equality & Discrimination

Economic
- Innovation
- Employment
- Changing business models
- Improved efficiency

Legal
- Security & Privacy
- Liability
- Intellectual Property Rights
- Accountability

Political
- Surveillance
- Participation
- Decision making
- Political Abuse

Figure 1.5　Impact of big data analytics.

1.8 Impact of Big Data

Making use of big data analytics in their processes has highly impacted different industries. These impacts can be categorized as social and ethical impact, economic impact, legal impact and political impact (Figure 1.5).

References

Bulao, J. (2022, 10 13). *How much data is created every day in 2022?* techjury.net. Retrieved from https://techjury.net/blog/how-much-data-is-created-every-day/

Khan N., Husain, M. S., & Beg, M. R. (2015). Big data classification using evolutionary techniques: A survey. *IEEE International Conference on Engineering and Technology (ICETECH)* (pp. 243–247).

Khan, N., & Husain, M. S. (2017). Big data on E-government. In S. Zoughbi (Ed.), *Securing government information and data in developing countries* (pp. 27–36). IGI Global.

Mohammad Shahid Husain, M. Z., & Khan, M. Z. (2019). *Critical concepts, standards, and techniques in cyber forensics.* IGI Global.

Prodanoff, J. T. (2022, 10 07). *How much data is created every day in 2022.* webtribunal.net. Retrieved from https://webtribunal.net/blog/how-much-data-is-created-every-day/

Statista Research Department. (2022, 9 8). *Amount of data created, consumed, and stored 2010–2020, with forecasts to 2025.* statista.com. Retrieved from https://www.statista.com/statistics/871513/worldwide-data-created/

Vuleta, B. (2021, 10 28). *How much data is created every day? +27 staggering stats.* Retrieved from https://seedscientific.com/: https://seedscientific.com/how-much-data-is-created-every-day/

Chapter 2

Challenges of Big Data

2.1 Introduction

In the recent past, big data has become a hotspot facilitating a pool of emerging tools and technologies to support huge volumes of data storage and analytics in many business application domains. As big data technologies are developing at a rapid pace, more and more organizations are gearing up to embrace big data as a core component of their information management and analytics infrastructure.

However, the true implementation of a big data platform has many complications. These obstacles require quick attention and must be addressed properly, since if they are not resolved, the technology may fail, which can have undesirable consequences.

The following are some of the challenges that need to be tackled in big data implementation:

- Big data integration
- Storing big data
- Maintaining data quality
- Analysis of big data
- Security management
- Privacy issues

DOI: 10.1201/9781003441595-3

2.2 Big Data Integration

One of the key advantages of big data analytics is that organizations can acquire data from incongruent sources and merge and explore them to get valuable insights as per their business needs. Although it looks quite simple, due to its inherent features big data tends to be mostly unstructured and we need to implement comprehensible integration processes.

2.2.1 Issues in Data Integration

■ Users should have good knowledge of where the required information is stored and how it can be accessed.
■ Representation of the same entity in different data sources can be different. The same term in different data sources can refer to different entities.

2.2.2 Approach to Data Integration

The below steps should be followed properly while accessing multiple datasets. A mistake in any of these steps can lead to inefficient data processing or failure to get the required result.

■ Decide which data sources should be used
■ Divide query into sub-queries to the data sources
■ Decide in which order to send sub-queries to the data sources
■ Send sub-queries to the data sources – use the terminology of the data sources
■ Merge results from the data sources to get an answer to the original query

2.2.3 Data Integration Methods

Unifying unstructured data for storage and analysis purposes is one of the most critical hurdles faced by organizations in implementing big data.

There are three common methods for data integration:

■ Link-driven federations
■ Warehousing
■ Mediation or view integration: A global schema is defined over all data sources

2.2.3.1 Link-Driven Federations

Link-driven federations provide explicit links between data sources. The queries provide interesting results by using web links to reach related data in other data sources. These web links are explicitly created by the developers based on organizational needs. In the worst case, we need indexes between every pair of databanks. In practice, the difference is made between directly and indirectly linked databanks.

The link-driven federation approach is not commonly used in most business domains because it requires good knowledge of data sources and also because its implementation is complicated because of syntax-specific commands.

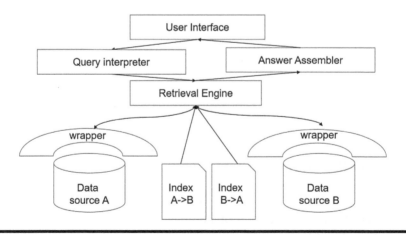

Figure 2.1   Link-driven federation data integration architecture.

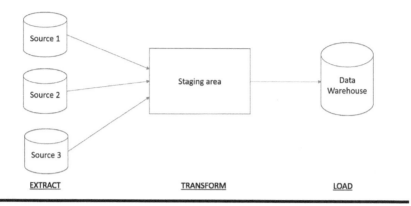

Figure 2.2   Data warehousing architecture.

2.2.3.2 *Warehousing*

This is the most popular traditional method of data integration. Data is downloaded, filtered, integrated and stored in a warehouse following the extract, transform and load (ETL) process. ETL defines the extract, transform and load steps of data integration. The ETL is an automated process employed by organizations.

2.2.3.2.1 Extract

In this phase, the data is extracted from different sources like enterprise resource planning (ERP), web pages, emails, SQL servers, NoSQL servers, CRMs, etc.

2.2.3.2.2 Transform

In the data staging area, the data is processed and transformed to make it analysis-ready as per business needs. The main functions applied at this stage are data preprocessing, cleaning, translation, summarization, calculations to get derived parameters, unit conversions, etc.

2.2.3.2.3 Loading

All the data ready for analysis is loaded in the warehouse. After that periodic loading is performed to maintain the changes and update the warehouse data.

ETL is a time-consuming batch operation, which is effective more often for creating smaller target data repositories that require less frequent updating.

2.2.3.3 Mediation

In the mediation method of data integration, a global schema is defined over the data sources. A high-level query language is used to perform translation between the global schema and the schemas of the local data sources.

As shown in Figure 2.3, mediation architecture consists of the following components:

- Ontology base: Provides context-based semantics to the data items.
- Databank knowledge base: Provides information about the contents and capabilities of the source databanks including the schema/conceptual model, information about data distribution, queries, etc.
- Mediator: The central system, comprised of
  - The query interpreter and expander: Expands queries using ontologies.
  - The retrieval engine: Generates a query plan.

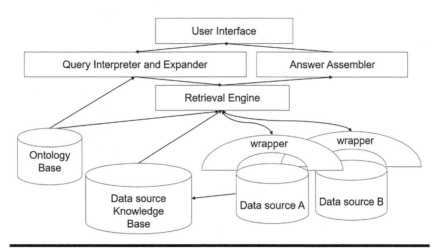

Figure 2.3   Mediation architecture for data integration.

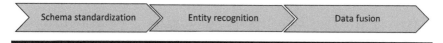

| Schema standardization | Entity recognition | Data fusion |

Figure 2.4   Big data integration stages.

- Divides global query into sub-queries.
- Optimization (which sub-queries are sent to which data source and in which order).
- Uses database knowledge base.
  - The answer assembler: Arranges query results for presentation.
■ Wrappers: Translators between the language/schema in the central system and the languages/schema in source databases, internal retrieval systems.
■ Source databanks: These are accessible through wrappers.

Generally, the mediation approach is implemented in three stages as shown in Figure 2.4.

2.2.3.3.1 Schema Standardization

The data acquired from multiple internal and external sources with different or no schemas needs to be aligned in a standard schema. The first step in this process is the creation of a mediated schema that provides a uniform structure given to all data sources. After that attribute matching is done based on the schema dimensions. Finally, the original data source schema is mapped with the mediated schema using a GAV, LAV or BAV scheme.

■ Global as view (GAV) – the global schema is defined in terms of source terminology. Mapping gives direct information about which data satisfies the global schema.
■ Local as view (LAV) – the schema of data sources is defined in terms of the global schema. It specifies how to find data in the original source via the global schema.
■ Both as view (BAV) – it allows two-way querying between the global schema and original source and vice versa.

2.2.3.3.2 Entity Resolution

This stage involves activities like redundancy removal, named entity recognition, ambiguity resolution, etc.

- Redundancy removal – removes the duplicated data.
- Entity recognition – recognizes the same entities with different representations in different data sources. It also identifies the entities which are different but have the same representation in different data sources.
- Ambiguity resolution – provides the most suitable semantic to a data item with multiple interpretations based on the context.

2.2.3.3.3 Data Fusion

We have huge sets of data sources available to acquire data, but not all data contains accurate and usable information. The fusion of online data from various sources to discover the correct data for storage needs to maintain the data quality and data veracity.

2.3 Storing Big Data

Identifying the options available and selecting the optimum solution for storing massive amounts of data in an organizational setting is vital. Big data analytics is beneficial only when organizations can manage to store the vast amount of available data. This compels organizations to build the capacity to store and manage datasets that are effectively infinite in size.

In spite of the developments in storage technology that have resulted in enhanced performance and scalability, a conventional USB memory stick or an external hard drive will not be adequate to store the necessary information in the context of big data analytics. With the advent of Internet technologies, data generation has increased at a rate that is exponential which creates the requirement of data storage with the increased capability to handle large datasets.

Essentially, the most crucial requirements of big data storage are the ability to manage very large amounts of data and the ability to continue scaling to keep up with data growth regardless of the size of the organization or the sector in which it operates because even small size organizations acquire a significant amount of data from a variety of sources which needs to be stored somewhere before it can be processed.

This storage should not only facilitate the storage of massive volumes of data but also be able to accommodate both structured and unstructured data and handle high rates of random write and read access. Another critical aspect for organizations is to put proper measures in place to ensure the security of the data storage.

2.3.1 Big Data Storage Methods

The two widely used storage solutions for large amounts of data are as follows.

2.3.1.1 Data Warehouse

When it comes to storing and processing data on an enterprise level, nothing beats a data warehouse. Its role is comparable to that of a traditional warehouse, which is used for the storage of physical items. These warehouses store the archival data or the historical data along with the day-to-day transactional data of an organization which facilitates a wide variety of operations like reporting, business intelligence, analytics, data mining, research, cyber monitoring, predictive analysis, etc. Data warehouse solutions facilitate efficient data management by making it simple to discover, retrieve, visualize and analyze information.

The capability to transform raw data into useful business knowledge and provide insights to decision makers with different perspectives is the most valuable advantage that comes with using a data warehouse along with its low cost and ease of implementation.

2.3.1.2 Storage in the Cloud

Another alternative for storing massive volumes of data is cloud storage, which is gaining in popularity in recent times. As opposed to physically storing data on a hard drive or computer, cloud storage allows you to save your data and information online and access it from any device, from anywhere in the world (Husain & Khanum, 2017).

As a part of a cloud computing environment, cloud storage is an on-demand service which can be used to save an almost inexplicably enormous amount of data online and access it from anywhere anytime. This option of data storage is more popular because it does not demand huge investment in building the in-house storage infrastructure; even small/medium size organizations can use cloud storage by only paying the service provider as per their usage. It also provides flexibility in scaling up and down their storage capacity as per their needs.

Businesses have also benefited greatly from on-demand cloud storage service because of the simplicity with which employees can access, share and update information regardless of their physical location.

2.4 Maintaining Data Quality

The accuracy of any business intelligence system depends on the quality of data to be used for data analytics. Quality data means accurate, authentic, complete, consistent and timely acquired datasets which serve the organizational business purpose. Data quality (DQ) is a critical component of big data analytics as the data is acquired from multiple sources most of which are unstructured sources like the world wide web and social media platforms where there is no standard data format and no assurance of the quality of data.

2.4.1 Data Quality Dimensions

Ikbal Taleb et al. suggested some data quality dimensions to measure, quantify and manage data quality. Each of these quality dimensions has specific metrics to measure the data quality standard (Taleb et al., 2021). These quality dimensions are grouped into four categories as shown in Figure 2.5. Out of the four categories, the intrinsic data qualities and contextual data quality parameters which are summarized in Table 2.1 are the most critical.

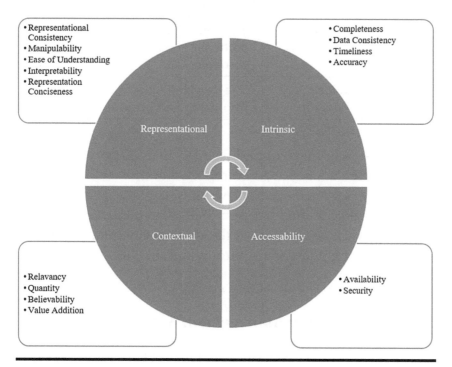

Figure 2.5   Big data quality dimensions.

Table 2.1 Big Data Intrinsic and Contextual Quality Dimensions

Category	DQ Dimension	Description
Intrinsic	Completeness	Records should be complete. Missing values should be handled properly.
	Consistency	The data values should be consistent throughout the database.
	Timeliness	The data should be available and accessible when it is needed.
	Accuracy	How well does a data item reflect the realistic values?
Contextual	Relevancy	The data should be relevant to the information needs.
	Quantity	The dataset should be of standard size for effective analysis. Small sample sizes generally lead to inaccurate information for decision making.
	Believability	The data collected should be authentic and from verifiable resources.
	Value Addition	The data should provide valuable information for business purposes.

Before storing the acquired data for analysis purposes the quality of the data needs to be reported and verified. A big data quality management framework is used for data quality evaluation and not only helps in improving the data preprocessing activities to strengthen the data quality but also facilitates monitoring and control throughout the lifecycle of big data.

2.4.2 Data Quality Management Steps

Data quality management will generally be composed of the following components (Profisee Data Quality, 2022):

- **Data governance framework**: This framework provides the data rules and standards for measuring the data quality based on the organizational needs.
- **Data profiling**: During data profiling, the data governance team members evaluate data assets and identify the relevant data items based on the current information needs. Data profiling also helps in choosing the optimum steps and measures to ensure data quality.
- **Data matching**: In this stage, the same entities with different representations are identified. Data matching helps in entity recognition and deduplication which reduces the size of the dataset for analysis by removing the redundancies.
- **Data reporting**: Data reporting is the process of reporting all of the data quality dimensions with their measured values. These reports help data governance team members in taking measures for improving the data quality.
- **Data repair/enrichment**: Data repair and enrichment is the process of enhancing the quality of the dataset by confirming that quality standards are being adhered to and providing supplementary contextual information if required.
  - Master data management (MDM): An MDM framework is used to store metadata after data profiling and data matching. This helps in avoiding the repetition of data cleaning and preprocessing.
  - Customer data integration (CDI): CDI helps in ensuring the data quality while integrating customer data from multiple sources like CRM, registration or feedback.
  - Product information management (PIM): PIM helps different stakeholders like product manufacturers, suppliers, merchants, distributors, etc., to maintain data quality using standard quality indicators across supply chain management (SCM).

2.5 Analysis of Big Data

Realizing the vital benefits of big data, more and more orga-nizations are putting effort into collecting as much data as they can. However, simply collecting and storing large amounts of data isn't enough; to get usable insights, this data has to be analyzed by implementing appropriate methods. The goal of big data analytics is to analyze large datasets for recurring patterns and relationships using sophisticated technologies in addition to the traditionally used statistical analysis techniques in order to support data-driven decision making.

The analysis of big data presents a number of significant issues, the most important of which are:

■ Determining how to address a problem in the case of excessively vast volumes of data.
■ Determining which data points are the most important.
■ Determining ways to make the most of the information in hand.

2.5.1 Working Principle of Big Data Analytics

The process of procuring, integrating, processing, transform-ing and analyzing large volumes of data to facilitate big data implementation is referred to as big data analytics. The follow-ing are the steps involved in big data analytics.

2.5.1.1 Setting the Goal

Big data analytics can uncover many hidden patterns and trends which can provide beneficial insights for deci-sion making. However, the first step in data analytics is to clearly define the specific business objectives behind the analysis.

2.5.1.2 Identification of Data

It is critical to have good knowledge about the available data sources. Identifying the relevant data sources which can provide the data as per business needs is crucial.

2.5.1.3 Data Preprocessing

Data is preprocessed and cleaned to make it usable as per organizational needs. This step involves operations like handling missing values, deduplication and entity recognition.

2.5.1.4 Data Transformation

Data is transformed into forms appropriate for analysis purposes by performing operations like summarization and aggregation.

2.5.1.5 Data Integration

The data collected from a variety of sources is integrated and stored in a data warehouse or any other big data storage platform.

2.5.1.6 Data Analysis

Traditional analytical and statistical tools along with intelligent methods like data mining and deep learning are applied to extract hidden data patterns and relations. These patterns are evaluated to identify the truly interesting patterns representing knowledge based on interestingness measures.

2.5.1.7 Data Visualization and Reporting

Different knowledge representation and data visualization techniques are used to represent the information extracted in a graphical representation and reported to the stakeholders for decision making.

2.6 Security and Privacy Management

In recent years, technological advances and novel applications, such as smart mobile devices, social networks, cloud computing environments, sensor networks, IoT and cyber-physical systems, have made it possible to collect, store and process gigantic amounts of data about everything from everywhere and at any time using the Internet.

Although organizations are enjoying the benefits of big data analytics, they are facing one of the most critical challenges in terms of securing this vast amount of data and maintaining data privacy.

2.6.1 Need for Data Protection

In recent years, privacy issues and data breaches have made headlines across social media. These stories have served as a warning to users. Companies that manage vast amounts of sensitive information are more vulnerable to data leaks and privacy difficulties, while consumer privacy rules such as GDPR (Regulation, GDPR General Data Protection, 2016) are falling short in their ability to protect individuals' privacy. Customers have reasonable concerns about the privacy of their personal data in this day and age of digital technology.

Information is one of the most valuable assets for any organization. According to the information security framework (ISO/IEC 27001, 2022), organizations should implement data protection measures to ensure the CIA triad, i.e. confidentiality, integrity and availability. Risks associated with privacy like data breaches, data brokerage and data discrimination should be identified and handled carefully. Those organizations who make data protection a top priority not only earn the loyalty of customers by showing respect for individuals' right to privacy, but they also safeguard their own long-term interests by cultivating a company culture that places a premium on informed decision making and the protection of individuals' personal information.

2.6.2 Challenges in Protecting Big Data

- With the increase in unstructured data and non-relational database systems it is becoming more challenging to guarantee the security of the data.
- Generally big data platforms are cluster-based, which exposes many nodes and servers to a wide range of vulnerabilities.
- The use of advanced systems like cloud, IoT, sensors, etc., for collecting and storing data has opened new avenues for attacks and security threats.
- Due to its potentially enormous size (terabytes to pet-abytes), performing routine security checks is tricky.
- Owners of big data put themselves at risk of data loss and disclosure if the security of the environment is not consistently maintained.
- The professionals who protect large amounts of data need to be skilled in cleansing and understand how to remove malware.

2.6.3 Best Practices for Big Data Protection

- The use of encryption techniques like Advanced Encryption Standard (AES) and Hashed Message Authentication Code (HMAC) can maintain end-to-end encryption and provide security.
- Signed message digests should be used to assign an encrypted unique identification to each digital data file.
- Organizations should implement measures like secure untrusted data repository (SUNDR) to identify

unauthorized file modifications caused by hostile server agents.

■ To counter Sybil attacks and ID-spoofing attacks, end-point filtering and validation should be employed to allow only trusted devices to connect to the network. This can be done by using trusted credentials, statistical similarity detection and outlier detection algorithms for verifying resources.

■ Big data platform administrators might collect information without seeking consent or giving notification. Any dubious access, whether for legitimate or malicious reasons, must be detected and flagged by the monitoring program.

■ Granular access control can be implemented, i.e. providing data access only to authorized users as per business needs.

■ A single sign-on system that only requires one password can be utilized, and things should always be labelled correctly.

■ Granular auditing is absolutely necessary for big data protection, which helps organizations to respond more quickly to an event by creating a single audit perspective after an attack and reducing the number of audit records generated and minimizing unnecessary audits.

■ The security and privacy of audit logs should not be ignored. Data used for auditing purposes should be kept in a secure location, safeguarded by strict access controls and reported on at regular intervals. An orchestrator tool such as ElasticSearch can be used to ensure that big data and audit data are kept completely separate and to enable all logging that is required.

■ Applications that work with big data generate something called provenance metadata. This is a new kind of data that needs to be protected in a particular manner. Establishing an infrastructure authentication mechanism that not only governs access but also configures daily status alerts and continuously verifies data integrity using checksums is a necessary step.

■ Monitoring big data in real time helps organizations to stay on top of potential data breaches and enables you to execute data security policies in a timelier and effective manner.

■ In order to provide the highest level of protection for their customers' individual privacy, businesses should carefully assess the possibility of erasing any personal information that is no longer required.

2.7 Accessing and Sharing Information

Data can facilitate effective information generation and decision making only if it is accessed or shared in a complete, accurate and timely manner. The inaccessibility of datasets required from external sources is likely the most common obstacle that must be overcome in big data initiatives. The process of accessing and sharing data from external sources might be very complex and difficult. The requirement for legal documents to be shared is one of the variety of challenges organizations face in retrieving data from external repositories.

References

Regulation, GDPR General Data Protection. (2016). *Complete guide to GDPR compliance. online: GDPR. eu*< https://gdpr.eu

Husain, M. S., & Khanum, M. A. (2017). Cloud computing in E-governance: Indian perspective. In Saleem Zoughbi (Eds). *Securing government information and data in developing countries* (pp. 104–114). IGI.

ISO/IEC 27001. (2022). *Information security, cybersecurity and privacy protection — Information security management systems — Requirements.* International Standards Organization (ISO). Retrieved from https://www.iso.org/standard/82875.html

Jin, X., Wah, B. W., Cheng, X., & Wang, Y. (2015). Significance and challenges of big data research. *Big Data Research*, *2*(2), 59–64.

Profisee Data Quality. (2022). *Profisee master data management (MDM)*. profisee.com. Retrieved from https://profisee.com/data-quality-what-why-how-who/

Taleb, I., Serhani, M. A., Bouhaddioui, C., & Dssouli, R. (2021). Big data quality framework: A holistic approach to continuous quality management. *Journal of Big Data*, *8*(1), 1–41.

Chapter 3

Big Data Analytics

3.1 Introduction

Big data analytics refers to the complex process of analyzing a large-volume of datasets to discover hidden patterns and relations and providing useful insights to decision makers for effective strategy planning as per business needs.

Big data analytics involves the use of sophisticated tools and techniques for cleaning, integrating and processing huge volumes of data in hand and visualizing the important insights for decision making.

These statistics make use of the data that you already have and make educated assumptions to fill in any gaps in the data that remains. They combine historical data found in enterprise resource planning (ERP), customer relationship management (CRM), human resources (HR) and point of sale (POS) systems in order to recognize patterns in the data. They then apply statistical models and algorithms in order to capture relationships between different datasets.

DOI: 10.1201/9781003441595-4

3.2 Applications of Big Data Analytics

The potential rewards of getting data analytics right and transforming the organization into a data-driven organization are substantial. Organizations that have optimized their supply chain, reduced their operational expenses, boosted their revenues or enhanced their customer service and product mix can earn enormous returns on their investments.

3.2.1 Traditional Business Applications of Big Data Analytics

Big data analytics is nothing new. Traditional businesses (as shown in Figure 3.1) like manufacturing, financial services, fraud detection, etc., have used data analytics in one form or another for a long time.

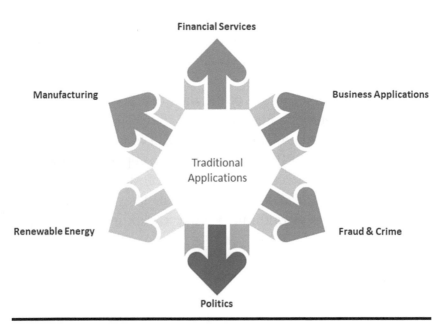

Figure 3.1 Traditional business applications of big data analytics.

3.2.1.1 Manufacturing

In the manufacturing industry, big data analytics is used for the following:

- Product quality control
- Revenue performance
- Maintenance forecasting

3.2.1.2 Financial Services

Financial service industries use big data analytics for the following purpose:

- Stock exchange prediction
- Credit score-based loan/credit card approval
- Risk analysis

3.2.1.3 Business Applications

Business applications use big data analytics for better:

- Customer profiling
- Supply chain management
- Targeted marketing
- Logistics
- E-commerce
- CRM

3.2.1.4 Fraud and Crime

Fraud and crime control agencies use big data analytics to identify and counter:

- Financial fraud
- Tax evasion
- Criminal activities

3.2.1.5 Politics

In politics, big data analytics is useful for:

■ Identifying ideological bias
■ Trend analysis
■ Evaluation of public reactions

3.2.1.6 Renewable Energy Sector

In the renewable energy sector, big data analytics is very useful in:

■ Energy forecasting
■ Predictive maintenance
■ Effective pricing

3.2.2 Recent Application Trends in Big Data Analytics

As industries are realizing the benefits of making use of huge volumes of data available through big data analytics more and more businesses are turning towards its implementation. The advancement in sophisticated techniques and advanced machine learning models has also helped organizations to incorporate big data analytics in their regular functioning. The latest trends in big data analytics include applications like healthcare, education, sports, cybercrime, etc., as shown in Figure 3.2.

3.2.2.1 Healthcare

Healthcare is one of the areas in recent times that has made the best use of the big data analytics framework. Using data analytics can improve the healthcare sector in multiple ways like:

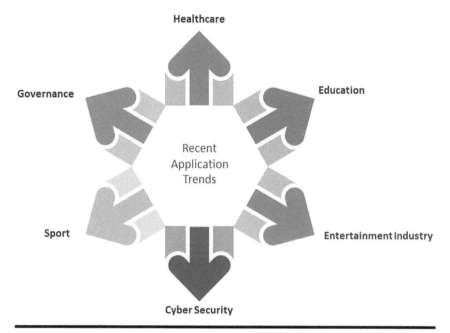

Figure 3.2   Latest trends in big data analytics.

■ Early diagnosis
■ Identifying patients more vulnerable to chronic diseases
■ Pervasive healthcare
■ Predicting pandemics and health issues

3.2.2.2 Education Sector

Education is another sector where big data analytics can impact on decision making for:

■ Enrollment
■ Retention
■ Budgeting
■ Self-learning
■ Student monitoring
■ Collaborative learning

- Pedagogical support
- Welfare support

3.2.2.3 Entertainment Industry

Entertainment industries like Netflix and Amazon are making use of big data analytics to understand their customer base and improve their services like:

- Customer satisfaction and retention
- Personalized recommendations
- Criminal activities

3.2.2.4 Cyber Security

Most organizations and individuals don't know how to identify and tackle illegal activities going on in the cyber world as they are generally unaware of the cyber laws and sophisticated techniques to counter these attacks. Big data analytics can help organizations in taking proper measures against these security breaches by:

- Analyzing fraudulent activity
- Monitoring suspicious financial activities

3.2.2.5 Sport

Big data analytics in the sports industry is one of the latest trends where analysts can make use of vast amounts of data about players, teams, playing conditions and so on for:

- Player, team and fan management analysis
- Structuring player contracts
- Avoiding mishaps

3.2.2.6 E-Governance

Big data analytics can help in effective governance in the following ways:

- Preparing for natural disasters
- Countering terrorism
- Preventing child abuse and fatalities
- Policy making

3.3 Types of Big Data Analytics

Examining all of the available analytic choices can be a challenging task. Fortunately, these different approaches to data analysis can be broken down into four broad categories at a high level. There is no one method of analysis that is superior to any other, and in reality, all of them co-exist with one another and complement one another.

The four levels of big data analytics (as shown in Figure 3.3) are descriptive, diagnostic, predictive and prescriptive analytics.

3.3.1 Descriptive Analytics

When you require a bird's-eye view of your company's activities and when you want to sum up and characterize various aspects of your business, descriptive analytics is the way to go. Descriptive analysis as the name suggests is used to describe, or summarize, raw data so that it may be comprehended by humans. Descriptive analytics is statistical in nature and describes the events happening. Descriptive analytics provides insights indicating things like inventory totals, consumer spending averages year-over-year sales fluctuations, etc., and is helpful for effective decision making. Descriptive analytics

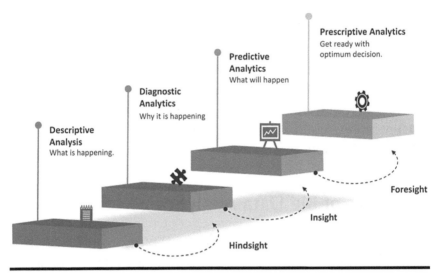

Figure 3.3   Types of big data analytics.

is commonly used in management reporting to analyze past production, finances, operations, sales, finances, inventory and customers' responses.

Descriptive analytics uses statistical methods like adding, subtracting, averaging and calculating percentage changes on a particular data field to describe the situation like whether the sale of the new product has increased or decreased. Measures like segregation, discrimination and inequality are studied using specialized descriptive techniques. Discrimination is measured with the help of audit studies or decomposition methods.

Some of the widely used statistical methods for descriptive analytics are as follows.

3.3.1.1 Measures of Frequency

Measures like count, percent and frequency are used to see how often something occurs.

3.3.1.2 Measures of Central Tendency

These measures locate the distribution of various data points. Measures like mean, median and mode are used to find an average or most commonly indicated response.

3.3.1.3 Measures of Dispersion or Variation

These measures identify the spread of data values by stating intervals. Measures like range (high–low), variance and standard deviation are used to show how "spread out" the data values are.

3.3.1.4 Measures of Position

These measures describe how data items are related to one another. Measures like percentile ranks and quartile ranks are used on normalized data values to compare them with standardized values.

3.3.2 Diagnostic Analytics

Descriptive analytics gives you answers to questions like whether the sale of the new product has increased or decreased. But it can't satisfactorily answer questions like why sales are going down or why the performance of employees decreased during the past month.

Diagnostic analytics offers analytical capabilities like data discovery, data mining, data correlation and drill-down through which users can diagnose the data in hand and identify possible reasons/sources for the abnormalities (unexpected changes in performance) by drilling further down into the data.

Diagnostic analytics allows analysts to explore trends both within the organizational data and outside sources of data in order to arrive at a conclusion that is more informed. The fields of probability theory, filtration, analytics for regression and time series data analysis are all examples of important techniques utilized in diagnostic analytics.

3.3.3 Predictive Analytics

After getting to know what is happening and why it's happening, the third step for a successful business is to know what will happen.

Most organizations have already implemented and utilize descriptive analytics and diagnostic analytics. Now the trend is towards more and more organizations adopting predictive analytics.

Predictive analytics refers to advanced analytical strategies that allow us to predict future trends and outcomes based on the discovered patterns by using sophisticated AI and machine learning techniques along with statistical methods like regression analysis. Predictive analytics provides useful information to businesses that they may put to use. The use of predictive analytics allows for the estimation of the probability of a future outcome including what-if-then-else scenarios and risk analysis (Kumar, 2018).

It is essential to keep in mind that no system can "predict" the future with a degree of accuracy equal to or greater than 100%. These predictive analytics methods are used by businesses to make predictions about what might occur in the future. This is due to the fact that probabilities serve as the cornerstone around which predictive analytics are built.

When businesses need a glimpse into the future, they turn to predictive analytics. The application of predictive analytics may be found in all facets of a company, including the forecasting of consumer behavior and purchase patterns as well as the identification of trends in sales operations. They also provide support in estimating future needs for supply chain, operations, inventory inputs, projecting year-end revenue and speculating on which products buyers will buy together. The financial services industry uses credit ratings to predict whether or not a customer will pay back borrowed money on time in the future.

Through the use of application-level data, predictive analytics may forecast a client's future risk behavior, hence streamlining the customer acquisition process. Predictive analytics can help health insurance companies anticipate future costs by looking at a patient's medical claims history and, if accessible, their laboratory, pharmacy and other medical records. Predictive analytics can aid in underwriting these sums by estimating the likeliness of occurrences like illness, default, insolvency, etc. (Husain, 2019).

Organizations and businesses might benefit from doing predictive analyzes to foresee potential risks (Verma et al., 2018) and the consequences of natural disasters. They can make better decisions at the right moment with the aid of risk management.

The use of predictive analytics can assist in the identification of prospective customers, and it can also assist in determining the most effective combination of product variants, marketing content, communication channels and timing that should be utilized in order to target a certain consumer.

In an environment where the number of competing services is growing, businesses need to continually focus on ensuring that their customers are satisfied. When utilized appropriately, predictive analytics has the potential to lead to an active retention strategy by periodically analyzing the consumption, spending and behavior patterns of existing customers.

Predictive analytics enables us to determine which people have a greater likelihood of getting particular diseases, such as diabetes, asthma or a sickness that lasts a lifetime. This enables us to take precautions and give our patients higher-quality care.

3.3.3.1 Predictive Models

Based on the business needs and the datasets available, analysts use different types of models for prediction purposes.

3.3.3.1.1 Forecast Models

Forecast models are generally used to predict outcomes regarding sales, supply and demand, consumer behavior, etc.

3.3.3.1.2 Classification Models

Classification models are used to predict a predefined group for an unknown entity. For example, we can classify customers based on their credit ranking as to whether they will repay the loan or default.

3.3.3.1.3 Outlier Models

Outlier models are generally used to identify the anomalies in the datasets and figure out unwanted or unexpected activities like credit card fraud.

3.3.3.1.4 Time Series Models

Time series models are a kind of forecasting model where we make use of timestamped data to predict future events like share marketing prediction.

3.3.3.1.5 Clustering Models

Clustering models are based on unsupervised machine learning algorithms, where an unknown item is grouped based on similar characteristics, for example spam detection.

3.3.4 Prescriptive Analytics

Prescriptive analytics is a relatively new area that gives users the ability to "prescribe" a variety of possible courses of action and directs them to find the optimum solution in a given scenario. Organizations that have successfully implemented predictive analytics see prescriptive analytics as the next frontier (Lepenioti et al., 2020). Predictive analytics creates an estimate of what will happen next; prescriptive analytics tells you how to react in the best way possible given the prediction. In a nutshell, the provision of recommendations is the primary focus of these analytic efforts.

Prescriptive analytics is a branch of data analytics that uses predictive models to suggest actions to take for optimal outcomes. Prescriptive analytics relies on optimization and rules-based techniques for decision making. For example, forecasting the load on the electric grid over the next 24 hours is predictive analytics, whereas deciding how to operate power plants based on this forecast represents prescriptive analytics.

The goal of prescriptive analytics is to quantify the impact of potential future decisions in order to provide guidance on a range of potential outcomes prior to those decisions being implemented. Prescriptive analytics, in its most effective form, makes predictions not just about what will occur, but also about why it will occur, and it provides recommendations concerning actions that can be taken to take advantage of the predictions.

Prescriptive analytics goes further than descriptive and predictive analytics by making recommendations for one or more possible courses of action. In essence, it provides various predictions about the future and enables businesses to evaluate a number of different possible outcomes based on the activities they do. Prescriptive analytics integrates a number of methods and tools, including business rules, algorithms, machine learning (ML) and computational modeling processes.

Prescriptive analytics is being successfully used by larger companies to optimize production, scheduling and inventory in the supply chain. As a result, businesses have improved by enhancing the quality of their interactions with customers and assuring timely delivery of the correct products.

However, because of the complexities involved in implementing prescriptive analytics, the vast majority of businesses have not yet adopted this practice in their regular functioning.

3.4 Comparison of Data Analytics Stages

A robust analytic environment is required for an organization in order to be able to have a comprehensive picture of the market and to successfully compete within that market. This environment must comprise the following components.

Table 3.1   Comparison of Data Analytics Stages

Data Analytics	Data Processing	Findings	Outcome
Descriptive analytics	Learn from the historical data to provide insights using measures like frequency, central tendency and std. deviation	Describes the state of current business operations	Answer in terms of "What happened?"
Diagnostic analytics	Investigate primary issues by identifying anomalies present in the datasets	Highlights the reasons for different data trends	Answer in terms of "Why did it happen?"
Predictive analytics	Predict probable future outcomes by filling in the gaps in data	Creates different data models	Answer in terms of "What might happen?"
Prescriptive analytics	ML- and AI-based methods used to suggest variable-based outcome estimation	Suggests optimize outcomes	Answer in terms of "What should be done?"

The purpose of descriptive analytics is to answer the question "What has happened?" by gaining insight into the past through an aggregation of data from multiple sources and applying data mining techniques.

Techniques like data correlation and drill-down are used in diagnostic analytics to answer the question "why did it happen?" and identify possible reasons for the data trend.

The field of predictive analytics seeks to comprehend the future and provide a response to the question "What could happen?" by employing statistical models and forecasting methodologies.

In order to answer the question "What should we do?" and provide guidance on the many possible outcomes, prescriptive analytics employs optimization and simulation techniques.

References

Husain, M. S. (2019). Social Media Analytics to predict depression level in the users. In Sudip Paul, Pallab Bhattacharya, Arindam Bit (Eds.) *Early detection of neurological disorders using machine learning systems* (pp. 199–215). IGI Global.

Lepenioti, K., Bousdekis, A., Apostolou, D., & Mentzas, G. (2020). Prescriptive analytics: Literature review and research challenges. *International Journal of Information Management, 50,* 57–70.

Vaibhav Kumar, M. L. (2018). Predictive analytics: A review of trends and techniques. *International Journal of Computer and Applications, 182*(1), 31–37.

Verma, A., Arif, M., & Husain, M. S. (2018). Analysis of DDOS attack detection and prevention in cloud environment: A review. *International Journal of Advanced Research in Computer Science, 9,*107–113.

BIG DATA
TECHNOLOGIES

Chapter 4

Hadoop Ecosystem

4.1 Introduction

Big data analytics provides unlimited benefits to organizations. However, it comes with two crucial challenges: big data storage and big data processing. Big data cannot be handled using traditional techniques due to its inherent properties like volume, variety, velocity, etc. To handle this massive amount of data for storage and processing, we need a much more complex framework.

Some of the reasons why traditional systems fail to handle big data are:

- Traditional systems use in-house data storage and processing which are not suitable for storing and processing data from a number of different external sources.
- Traditional systems like relational databases are focused on structured data and inefficient in handling other formats like semi-structured and unstructured data.
- More investment is needed to improve in-house infrastructure to handle more and more data.

DOI: 10.1201/9781003441595-6

Table 4.1   Comparison between Traditional System and Hadoop Ecosystem

Traditional System	Hadoop Ecosystem
Less scalable	Highly scalable
Vertical scaling	Horizontal scaling
Less fault-tolerant	More fault-tolerant
More investment needed	Economical
Handles only structured data	Handles any type of data

The Apache™ Hadoop® project (Apache Software Foundation, 2006) facilitates open-source software for reliable, scalable, distributed computing. The Hadoop Ecosystem is an open-source framework, which facilitates the distributed storage and parallel processing of huge volumes of data across clusters of nodes or computers. The advantages of the Hadoop Ecosystem over traditional systems are summarized in Table 4.1.

4.2 Components of the Hadoop Ecosystem

Organizations face many challenges while handling big data such as acquiring and storing huge volumes of data, analyzing large datasets for information needs, searching and sharing data and the synchronization and control of activities.

The Hadoop Ecosystem facilitates all of these activities with ease by providing different components or tools.

The Hadoop Ecosystem is comprised of several key components which can be distributed across four layers based on the functionalities as shown in Figure 4.1.

4.2.1 Data Storage

The bottom layer of the Hadoop Ecosystem provides the facility to store large volumes of data in different formats including

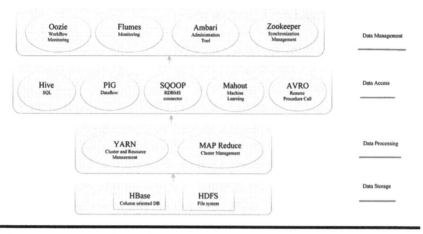

Figure 4.1   Layers in Hadoop Ecosystem.

structured, semi-structured and unstructured data. This layer uses two different components, one for mainly archived data and one for real-time data.

4.2.2 Data Processing

This layer provides tools to facilitate the parallel processing of big data. The components used in this layer are YARN and MapReduce.

4.2.3 Data Access

This layer provides different tools to facilitate access to the big data repository to elicit the information required as per the business need. The main components used in this layer are HIVE, PIG, SQOOP, Mahout and Avro.

4.2.4 Data Management

This layer provides tools to monitor, manage, control and synchronize the data and activities in the Hadoop Ecosystem. The main components used in this layer are Oozie, Flumes, Ambari and Zookeeper.

4.3 Data Storage Component

4.3.1 Google File System (GFS)

The Apache Hadoop framework is based on the Google File System (GFS). The GFS is a distributed system for handling large data files developed by Google. GFS is based on master slave architecture where we have one master server and many slave machines called chunk servers. The files to be stored are divided into chunks and stored on the chunk servers. To maintain data reliability, replicas of each file are stored on multiple chunk servers. The user can set the number of replicas to be stored as per requirements; by default the number of replicas to be stored is three. The master server maintains the metadata to perform activities like namespace monitoring and access control, mapping the requested file to the chunk, etc. (Ghemawat et al., 2003). The database used in GFS framework is Google Bigtable.

4.3.1.1 Bigtable

To store huge volumes of data in petabytes, GFS uses a scalable sparsely populated table which stores data in the form of a sorted key/value map. Bigtable is very efficient for storing different types of data like graphs, IoT data and time series data. For workload balance and effective query response, the content of the Bigtable is divided into different tablets. Each tablet is a block of contiguous rows. These tablets are stored on Google's internal, highly durable file system called Colossus, using storage devices in Google's data centers (Chang et al., 2006).

4.3.2 Hadoop Distributed File System (HDFS)

Hadoop's principal storage system is the Hadoop Distributed File System (HDFS). It's a distributed file system that works well with large data files and can be deployed on a cluster of inexpensive computers. The Hadoop Distributed File System is a core component in the Hadoop architecture which sits in the data storage layer in the Hadoop Ecosystem.

HDFS follows a master-slave architecture where the single master system is called the NameNode and the slave machines are called the DataNodes as shown in Figure 4.2. The NameNode and DataNode are software written in Java and can run on any commodity machine that supports Java. The HDFS architecture provides a file system namespace to store user data in equal sized chunks which are stored in different DataNodes (Borthakur, 2008).

4.3.2.1 NameNode

Every HDFS system has a single master server called the NameNode. The NameNode is responsible for managing the

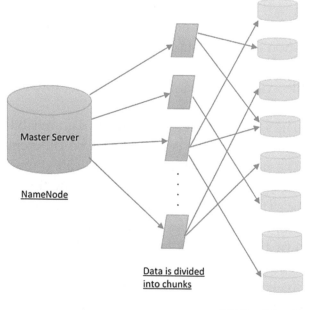

Figure 4.2   HDFS architecture.

file system namespace and allowing synchronized access to files by clients. The NameNode stores the metadata and performs operations like opening, closing and renaming files and directories. It also provides the mapping of chunk storages to DataNodes.

4.3.2.2 DataNode

The nodes that make up a Hadoop cluster and actually do the work are called DataNodes. They are utilized for the purpose of storing data chunks and transmitting these chunks to the clients in response to their read and write requests. The DataNodes also perform chunk creation, deletion and replication based on instructions from the NameNode.

4.3.2.3 Features of HDFS

The key features of the Hadoop Distributed File System are:

- Hierarchical file organization: HDFS provides a hierarchical organization to store data files. The HDFS architecture supports the creation of directories to store files. Just like any other file system, a user can create, move, rename or delete files.
- Reliability: The HDFS architecture ensures data reliability by maintaining duplicate copies of files on different machines. The number of duplicate copies, called the replication factor, is generally set by users at the time of configuration. The NameNode instructs the DataNodes to store the replicas of the files based on the replication factor given by the user. Rack-based automatic replication is a standard feature of the HDFS. DataNodes in the same rack save two copies of each block, while DataNodes in a different rack save the third copy of each block.
- Data integrity: To ensure data integrity, HDFS architecture uses the error checksum method. At the time of file

creation, the user generates the checksum for each chunk. When a user accesses a data file from any DataNode, the contents of the file are verified using the stored checksum. If the data is found to be corrupt, the user accesses the replicated copy of the file from another DataNode.

■ Robustness: HDFS provides a robust data storage architecture using Heartbeats and data re-replication. Each DataNode sends a periodic message called Heartbeat to the NameNode indicating that the DataNode is live and working fine. If a heartbeat is not received from a DataNode, the NameNode identifies that the node is dead and data files cannot be accessed from that node. Based on the replication factor, the NameNode performs the re-replication of data chunks.

HDFS architecture maintains a secondary NameNode apart from the primary or master NameNode. The secondary NameNode communicates with the primary NameNode periodically and copies the metadata to create checkpoints. If the primary NameNode crashes, these checkpoints on the secondary NameNodes are used for recovery.

4.3.2.4 Comparison between GFS and HDFS

HDFS is based on GFS and handles large data volumes consisting of a variety of data in a distributed framework. However, there are many differences between GFS and HDFS. Some of the key differences are summarized in Table 4.2.

4.3.3 HBase

To handle real-time, random huge-volume datasets, the Hadoop framework uses a non-relational and scalable distributed data management system that works on top of HDFS. Apache HBase provides Bigtable-like capabilities. HBase provides a fault-tolerant way of storing sparse datasets. The HBase

Table 4.2   GFS vs HDFS

Parameter	GFS	HDFS
Proprietary	GFS is a proprietary file system solely used by Google.	HDFS is an open-source file system which anyone can use.
Chunk size	In GFS, files are divided into fixed sized chunks of 64 MB to be replicated and stored on chunk servers.	In HDFS, files are divided into fixed sized blocks of 128 MB to be replicated and stored on DataNodes.
Communication protocol	GFS uses TCP connections to perform communication between chunks and clusters. Pipelining is used for data transfer.	TCP/IP protocol. Also uses Remote Procedure Call (RPC) for external communication between blocks and clusters.
Cache management	Cache metadata are saved in client's memory.	HDFS uses distributed cache files which can be private or publicly accessible.
Database	BigTable.	HBase.

provides the following features for effective real-time big data management (Apache HBase ™ Reference Guide, 2008):

- Supports high linear and modular scalability
- Consistent read and write operations
- Automatic and configurable splitting of large tables into blocks
- Robust
- Supports real-time queries using block caching and Bloom Filters

4.3.3.1 *Comparison between Bigtable and HBase*

Apache HBase is based on Google's Bigtable. Both are types of non-relational data storage for handling large volumes of datasets. However, there are some differences between Bigtable and HBase which are summarized in Table 4.3.

4.3.3.2 *Comparison between HDFS and HBase*

HBase is a top-level Apache project which runs on top of the HDFS. Some of the key differences between HDFS and HBase are summarized in Table 4.4.

Table 4.3   Bigtable vs HBase

Parameter	Bigtable	HBase
Proprietary	Bigtable is a proprietary system.	HBase is an open-source project.
Installation	Available only as a cloud service from Google.	Uses Apache Hadoop's HDFS as underlying storage and can be installed on any environment.
Concept	Bigtable is a three-dimensional mapping database that combines row key, column key and timestamp into a single byte array.	HBase is a column-oriented database.
Data integrity	Uses CRC checksum.	Uses checksum feature of HDFS.
Security management	Bigtable security relies on Google's Cloud Identity and Access Management.	Apache HBase uses Access Control Lists.
Timestamp	Timestamps in microseconds.	Timestamps in milliseconds.

Table 4.4   HDFS vs HBase

Parameter	HDFS	HBase
Concept	A file distribution system with rigid architecture.	HBase data storage runs on top of HDFS and supports dynamic changes.
Access method	Only sequential read/write operations. HDFS is based on write once read many times.	Random access using hash table. Supports random read and write operations into file system.
Data processing	Supports offline batch processing.	Efficient for real-time processing.
Latency	Provides high latency for access operations.	Provides low latency access to small amount of data.

4.4 Data Processing Component

4.4.1 MapReduce

Hadoop MapReduce is the main processing component of the Hadoop framework. It is based on the original MapReduce algorithm developed by Google and facilitates the distributed parallel processing of data. However, Google MapReduce can only work with the GFS file system whereas Hadoop MapReduce is a part of the Apache open-source project and is therefore used in many different architectures. Hadoop MapReduce has the ability to process large volumes of data, both structured and unstructured, and to manage very large data files in parallel by dividing the task into a number of independent jobs (MapReduce Tutorial, 2022).

MapReduce uses the divide and conquer approach for processing big data. It splits a task into multiple sub goals and processes them concurrently on different machines. Map

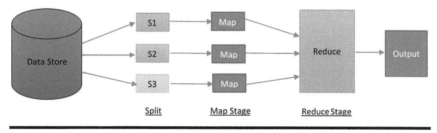

Figure 4.3 **MapReduce architecture.**

and reduce are the two stages in a MapReduce as shown in Figure 4.3.

- **Map stage**: Each map task executes different operations like filter, group, shuffle and sort on a split of input data on different machines simultaneously and generates a key-value pair.
- **Reduce stage**: The output of the map stage is acted upon by the reduce task where operations like aggregation and summarization are performed to generate the final result to be stored in HDFS.

4.4.2 YARN

YARN is the acronym of "Yet Another Resource Negotiator" and is a resource management component in Hadoop just like an operating system and works on top of the HDFS. In Hadoop 1.0, a JobTracker process was responsible for resource management, scheduling and the monitoring of job processing. Another process called TaskTrackers was used to perform individual map and reduce tasks and report back on their progress. Because this resource allocation and management was centralized at JobTracker, it created a performance bottleneck. Hence, YARN was created in Hadoop 2.0 to decentralize the task and alleviate this issue. The main role of YARN is to manage and allocate cluster resources and schedule the jobs with effective load balancing. In addition to this, it is also responsible for monitoring and the deployment of security controls. YARN assigns which tasks should be carried out by each node in the cluster and distributes the system resources necessary for each application that is running within a Hadoop cluster (Apache Hadoop YARN, 2022). YARN is made up of the following components as shown in Figure 4.4:

- **ResourceManager**: Jobs from the users are submitted to the ResourceManager which schedules these jobs and allocates resources to them.
- **NodeManager**: On every DataNode, NodeManager is installed which acts as a monitoring and reporting agent of the ResourceManager. These NodeManagers are responsible for monitoring resource usage including processing units, memory, disk storage and network capacities and reporting back to the ResourceManager.
- **ApplicationMaster**: Each application has a framework-specific library to negotiate resources based on the job

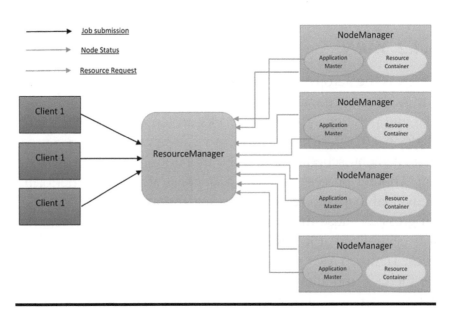

Figure 4.4   YARN architecture.

request from the ResourceManager and work with the NodeManager to execute and monitor tasks.

■ **ResourceContainers**: Each NodeManager has a component called the containers which contain a collection of resources including processing units, memory and disk storage. The ResourceContainers are controlled by NodeManagers and are used to assign the system resources allocated to individual applications.

4.4.2.1 Features of YARN

■ Dynamic allocation of system resources
■ Enables Hadoop real-time data processing along with MapReduce batch processing
■ Enhanced resource utilization and application performance
■ Supports various scheduling algorithms
■ Reservation feature enables users to reserve cluster resources in advance
■ Increased scalability with support from 10,000 to multiple tens of thousands of nodes

4.5 Data Access Component

4.5.1 Hive

Hive is an ETL and data warehousing tool developed by Apache. Hive makes it easier to query and manage massive datasets that are stored in multiple locations. Hive supports the summarization, querying and analysis of unstructured and semi-structured data in the Hadoop Ecosystem. The read, write and update operations on massive datasets in a distributed environment are performed through Hive Query Language (HQL) that is similar to Structured Query Language (SQL) and translates queries into MapReduce jobs automatically.

4.5.1.1 Components of Hive

- **Hive command line interface**: To execute HQL commands Hive provides a command line interface.
- **JDBC/ODBC driver**: For database connectivity, Java Database Connectivity (JDBC) and Object Database Connectivity (ODBC) drivers are used.

4.5.1.2 Hive Features

Some of the key features of Hive are:

- High scalability
- Real-time processing as well as batch query processing, i.e. interactive query processing
- Compatibility with each and every SQL primitive data type
- Support for user-defined functions (UDF) along with preset functions
- Automatic translation of queries into map and reduce functions through HQL
- Efficient extensive sequential scans

4.5.1.3 Limitations of Hive

- Not effective where fast response times are crucial because queries may encounter unusually high delays (up to several minutes).
- Hive is a read-based system and not suited for jobs typically involving many write operations.

4.5.2 Apache Pig

Pig is a platform for analyzing large datasets; it is comprised of a high-level language for describing data analysis programs and infrastructure for evaluating these programs.

Pig consists of two parts: Pig Latin, a programming language, and the Pig runtime, an environment in which Pig Latin programs can be executed. The ability of Pig programming to readily manage parallel processes gives it the advantage of being useful for managing very large amounts of data.

Pig supports the following scalar data types: int, float, double, long, chararray and bytearray. Pig's advanced data types are Map, Tuple and Bag.

Pig Latin is a straightforward scripting language that is similar in structure to SQL. Users find Apache Pig very comfortable as 200 lines of MapReduce Java code can be written in around 10 lines of Pig Latin. However, at a deeper level, the compiler translates Pig Latin into MapReduce. Pig Latin can be thought of as a black box which can easily generate a sequence of MapReduce jobs in an abstract way.

4.5.3 Apache Drill

Apache Drill is an open-source application that can perform analysis on massive datasets while working in a distributed context. Its main strength is to "drill" into the variety of NoSQL databases and file systems with only a single query. It offers a remarkable scalability factor, allowing it to support millions of users and serve their query requests for large-scale data in petabytes and exabytes.

4.5.4 Apache Sqoop

Apache Sqoop is a popular tool for the bidirectional data transfer of large datasets between Hadoop and relational database servers. It is a data migration tool based upon a connector architecture to connect with different databases. Sqoop uses JDBC driver which supports plugins to provide connectivity to a variety of external systems. Sqoop provides parallel data transfer which makes it fast and cost-effective. Sqoop can be used to import/export data from a wide variety of data stores, including but not limited to the following:

- HDFS
- Hive
- HBase
- Hcatalog
- Accumulo
- Oracle
- MySql
- PostgreSQL
- SQL Server
- DB2

4.5.5 Apache Avro

Developed by Doug Cutting, Apache Avro is an open-source remote procedure call and data serialization framework. Avro enables the interchange of large datasets between programs written in any language.

For ease of understanding, Avro uses the JSON format for representing data definition and binary format to store data itself making it compact and efficient. Avro files include markers for splitting data into subsets suitable for MapReduce.

4.5.5.1 Features of Avro

The key features of the Apache Avro framework are (Apache Avro™ 1.11.1 Documentation):

- Rich data structures
- A compact, fast, binary data format
- Robust support for dynamically changing data schemas
- A container file, to store persistent data
- Simple integration with dynamic languages including compiled and scripting languages

4.5.6 Apache Mahout

Apache Mahout is a framework to facilitate the free implementation of distributed and scalable machine learning algorithms focused primarily on linear algebra. For the concise and clear expression of algorithms, instead of traditional Scala-like syntax, Apache Mahout provides mathematically expressive Scala Domain Specific Language (DSL) which is similar to R syntax (Mahout, 2014).

Mahout offers data scientists a ready-to-use framework for performing the fast and effective analysis of large volumes of data using features like:

- Classification (using methods like distributed naive Bayes and complementary naive Bayes classification)
- Clustering (methods like k-means, fuzzy k-means, Canopy, Dirichlet and Mean-Shift)
- Recommendation
- Distributed fitness function capabilities for evolutionary programming
- Matrix and vector libraries

4.6 Data Management Component

4.6.1 ZooKeeper

Developed by the Apache Software Foundation, ZooKeeper is an open-source, centralized service that is responsible for coordinating numerous distributed services like managing configuration information, naming, distributed synchronization and delivering group services.

Before the introduction of ZooKeeper, coordinating amongst the various Hadoop Ecosystem services was an extremely challenging and time-consuming endeavor. Common configuration errors during data synchronization are just one example of the problems that have arisen in the past due to poor service interactions. Even if the services are configured, any modifications made to the configurations of the services will make it tough to manage. Additionally, item identification and categorization were time-consuming. ZooKeeper was developed as a solution to the issues mentioned. Just like any other distributed file system, ZooKeeper has a hierarchal name space with the only difference being that it allows a file to also be a directory (ZooKeeper Project, 2022).

4.6.1.1 Working of Apache ZooKeeper

A straightforward client server architecture serves as the foundation for ZooKeeper's overall design. The clients are the nodes that make service requests to the server, and the server is the node that fulfills those service requests on behalf of the clients. It's possible to have more than one ZooKeeper server. When the services are first begun, a chief administrator is chosen from within this community of servers. Every client establishes a connection with exactly one server, and that server alone is responsible for handling all of the read operations. Once a server receives a request to "write," it is sent on to the leader, who will then poll the quorum to see if it agrees with the action. A decision on this request needs to be approved by a quorum, which is defined as an absolute majority of the nodes that are part of the ensemble. If a favorable response is received from the quorum, the "write" request is judged to have been successful. This means that ZooKeeper is best suited for distributed systems with fewer "write" requests and more "read" ones, as the former take longer to process.

4.6.1.2 ZNode

The nodes in a ZooKeeper tree are referred to as ZNode. The responsibility of ZNode is to keep track of the statistics of the structure as well as the version numbers for any data updates.

Because ZooKeeper does not support partial read and write operations, the transactions are atomic.

4.6.1.2.1 Types of ZNodes

- **Persistent ZNodes**: This is the default ZNode. Only by making a call to Zookeeper's delete feature can it be removed from the system.
- **Ephemeral ZNodes**: These are the ZNodes with no child and get deleted along with the data stored when a session is ended or a connection is severed by the client.

4.6.2 Oozie

Apache Oozie is a scalable, reliable and extensible work-flow scheduler to manage Apache Hadoop jobs (Apache Oozie, 2021). As part of its architecture, Oozie uses a web server and a database to keep track of its various jobs. The default web server used in Oozie is the open-source software Apache Tomcat. The Oozie server is a stateless web application, which means that it does not retain any information in memory relating to the user or the job. When Oozie fetches the task state from the database in order to process the request, all of this information is first saved in the SQL database. The Oozie client can interact with the server in three distinct ways: via the command line tool, the Java Client API or the HTTP REST API.

4.6.3 Ambari

Apache Ambari provides an intuitive, easy-to-use Hadoop management web UI backed by its RESTful APIs. The highly interactive dashboard of Ambari facilitates keeping track of the running applications and their status in the easiest way. The goal of Ambari is to provision, manage and monitor Apache Hadoop clusters in the most effective way (Ambari, 2021).

4.6.3.1 Features of Ambari

- Easy step-by-step guide for installation and user-friendly configuration.
- The Ambari Metrics System provides immediate insight into the health of Hadoop clusters.
- The Ambari Alert Framework provides emergency alerts/notifications when a node goes down, disk space is low, etc.
- Central management for starting, stopping and reconfiguring Hadoop services across the entire cluster.
- Interactive dashboard for monitoring and visualizing the progress and status of every application running over the Hadoop cluster.
- Authentication, authorization and auditing by installing Kerberos-based Hadoop clusters.
- Flexible and adaptive technology.

4.6.4 Apache Flume

Flume is a service that efficiently collects, aggregates and moves enormous amounts of log data. It is a distributed system that is dependable and always available. Flumes provides a reliable and tolerant big data handling system with a number of failover and recovery techniques. It employs a straightforward data model that is capable of being extended, which makes online analytical applications possible (Apache Flume™, 2022).

4.6.4.1 Advantages of Apache Flume

- Flume facilitates a highly scalable, very dependable and highly fault-tolerant service.
- Flume ensures that there is a consistent flow of data transfer; for example, if the pace of reading data rises, then the speed of writing data will likewise increase.
- Because of its capacity to interface with a wide variety of applications, including Kafka, HDFS and Thrift, it provides a flexible option to users for data ingestion.

4.7 Apache Spark

Apache Spark is an alternative framework to Hadoop. Apache Spark is a software framework that is used to process data in a distributed manner and is replacing MapReduce in many use cases.

As a data processing engine, Apache Spark is known for its speed and ability to temporarily store its findings in memory space. It may be utilized in a broad variety of settings. Spark has numerous different deployment options. Apache Spark supports the programming languages Java, Python, Scala and R, and there is native assistance for SQL, real-time data (streaming data), machine learning (ML) and graph processing (GP) (Apache Spark™, 2014).

References

Ambari. (2021). ambari.apache.org. Retrieved from https://ambari .apache.org/

Apache Avro™ 1.11.1 Documentation. (n.d.). avro.apache.org. Retrieved from https://avro.apache.org/docs/1.11.1/

Apache Flume™. (2022). Retrieved from https://flume.apache.org/

Apache Hadoop YARN. (2022). hadoop.apache.org. Retrieved from https://hadoop.apache.org/docs/stable/hadoop-yarn/hadoop -yarn-site/YARN.html

Apache, HBase ™ Reference Guide. (2008). hbase.apache.org. Retrieved from https://hbase.apache.org/book.html

Apache Oozie. (2021). oozie.apache.org. Retrieved from https://oozie .apache.org/

Apache Software Foundation. (2006). *Apache Hadoop.* apache.org. Retrieved from https://hadoop.apache.org/

Apache Spark™. (2014). Retrieved from https://spark.apache.org/

Borthakur, D. (2008). *HDFS architecture guide.* hadoop.apache.o rg. Retrieved from https://hadoop.apache.org/docs/r1.2.1/hdfs _design.html

Chang, F., Dean, J., Ghemawat, S., Hsieh, W. C., Wallach, D. A., Burrows, M., Chandra, T., Fikes, A., & Gruber, R. E. (2006). Bigtable: A distributed storage system for structured data. *7th USENIX Symposium on Operating Systems Design and*

Implementation (OSDI), {USENIX} (pp. 205–218). cloud.google .com. Retrieved from https://cloud.google.com/bigtable/docs/ overview

Ghemawat, S., Gobioff, H., & Leung, S. T. (2003). The Google file system. *Proceedings of the nineteenth ACM symposium on operating systems principles* (pp. 29–43). ACM.

Mahout. (2014). mahout.apache.org. Retrieved from https://mahout .apache.org//

MapReduce Tutorial. (2022). hadoop.apache.org. Retrieved from https://hadoop.apache.org/docs/stable/hadoop-mapreduce-client/hadoop-mapreduce-client-core/MapReduceTutorial.html

ZooKeeper Project. (2022). *ZooKeeper: Because coordinating distributed systems is a zoo*. zookeeper.apache.org. Retrieved from https://zookeeper.apache.org/doc/r3.3.5/zookeeperOver.html

Chapter 5

NoSQL Databases

5.1 Introduction

NoSQL databases, referred to as "No SQL" or "Not only SQL," are non-tabular databases and store data differently than relational tables (IBM Cloud Education, 2019). The standard RDBMS system stores and retrieves information using SQL syntax for deeper analysis. This is done so that better choices can be made. Instead, data in a NoSQL database system can be stored in a wide variety of non-relational formats, such as structured, semi-structured, unstructured and polymorphic data, across several databases. A NoSQL database system is able to accommodate the storage of a variety of data. There is no requirement for a NoSQL database, also known as a non-relational data management system, to have a specified schema. NoSQL provides high scalability and availability, and because of this it is frequently utilized in environments dealing with large amounts of data as well as web applications that operate in real time, for example Twitter, Facebook and Google.

5.1.1 Features of NoSQL

RDBMS are the most widely used database management systems. However, with the exponential growth in the volume of

DOI: 10.1201/9781003441595-7   **81** data to be stored and managed, the reaction time of traditional RDBMS systems gradually slows down. It is possible that we will "scale up" our systems by adding additional hardware on top of what we already have in place in order to find a solution to this problem. This method comes at a very high financial cost.

Because of the massive volumes of data that Internet giants like Google, Facebook and Amazon, among others, are responsible for managing, the concept of NoSQL databases has received widespread acceptance. NoSQL supports the concept of "scaling out" where the burden of the database is distributed among several different servers when needed.

Some of the key features of NoSQL are as follows.

5.1.1.1 Non-Relational

NoSQL databases never adhere to the relational model. They don't produce tables with records that have a flat format and fixed column count. Data to be stored in NoSQL databases need not be normalized. Also, NoSQL doesn't support features like self-contained aggregates, BLOBs, referential integrity, specific query languages, query planners and BLOBs.

5.1.1.2 Schema Free

NoSQL databases can be defined as either having "schema-free" or "relaxed" schemas. It does not require any data structure explanation. NoSQL offers multiple file types for exchanging data that are all related to the same subject area.

5.1.1.3 Simple API

The most popular form of the NoSQL query language does not adhere to any particular industry standards databases that are enabled for the web and function as services that may be accessed via the Internet. Simple NoSQL APIs offer users storage and querying options for the data that has been provided, together with user interfaces that are basic and easy to understand and use. These APIs make it possible to do low-level activities such as processing data and selecting items from a list. Protocols are based on text and are frequently used in conjunction with HTTP, REST and JSON.

5.1.1.4 Distributed

The administration of large numbers of NoSQL databases can be performed in a decentralized approach which provides capabilities such as auto-scaling and failover. NoSQL is based on the "shared nothing" concept, i.e. the memory and disk spaces are not shared. As a direct consequence of this, there is a lower level of coordination and a greater degree of resource dispersion.

5.1.2 Difference between NoSQL and SQL

The key differences between SQL and NoSQL are summarized in Table 5.1.

5.2 Types of NoSQL Databases

Key-value pair databases, column-oriented databases, graph-based databases and document-oriented databases are the primary varieties of NoSQL databases. Every category has its own specific traits and requirements to fulfill. None of the databases presented here is preferable to the others when it comes to resolving all issues. Users need to select a database in accordance with the requirements of the product.

Table 5.1   Differences between SQL and NoSQL

Feature	SQL Databases	NoSQL Databases
Concept	SQL databases are relational databases used for structured data	NoSQL databases are non-relational databases used for storing unstructured data
Schema	SQL databases have a predefined schema and use structured query language	NoSQL databases have dynamic schemas suitable for unstructured data
Scalability	SQL databases are vertically scalable, i.e. handling the load by scale-up with a larger server	NoSQL databases are horizontally scalable, i.e. scale-out across commodity servers
Structure	SQL databases are table-based with fixed rows and columns	NoSQL databases are document, key-value, graph or wide-column stores
Preferable use	SQL databases are better for multi-row transactions	NoSQL is better for unstructured data like documents or JSON
Multi-record ACID transactions	Supported	Most NoSQL databases do not support multi-record ACID transactions. However, some – like MongoDB – do
Performance	Slow query processing compared to NoSQL	Generally, queries in NoSQL databases are faster than SQL databases
Joins	Required to perform various query operations	Joins are typically not required in NoSQL databases

5.2.1 Types of NoSQL Databases

■ Key-value pair based
■ Column-oriented databases
■ Document-oriented databases
■ Graph-based

5.3 Key-Value Pair Based Storage

Data is kept as pairs of keys and values. It is designed to handle large amounts of data and heavy loads. Key-value pair storage databases store data as a hash table in which each key is unique and the value can be a JSON object, BLOB, text, etc. In a sense, a key-value store is like a relational database with only two columns: the key or attribute name (such as "P-Id") and the value (such as "1023") as shown in Table 5.2.

This kind of NoSQL database can be used to store various data types, including collections, dictionaries, associative arrays and more. With the assistance of key-value stores, programmers can easily store data that does not have a schema. The contents of shopping carts are the primary beneficiaries of their utilization.

Key-value stores are primarily used for handling large amounts of data with simple lookup queries.

Table 5.2   Example of Key-Value Store

Key	Value
P-Id	1023
P-name	'abc'
Weight	153 kg
Height	143 cm

5.4 Column-Oriented Databases

The structure of column-oriented databases is based on Google's BigTable concept. In contrast to relational databases where data is stored in rows and accessed in a row-by-row fashion, a column-oriented database is organized as a set of columns. Just like key-value stores, column-oriented databases have some basic NoSQL structure while also preserving a lot of flexibility. In a single table column names and formatting can differ from row to row and each column is stored separately on disk. This means that when you want to run analytics on a small number of columns, you can read those columns directly without consuming memory with the unwanted data. The information contained in each column is processed individually and hence column-oriented databases can quickly aggregate the value of a given column. Columns are often of the same type and benefit from more efficient compression, making reads even faster. These characteristics of column-oriented databases make it very useful for analyzing large amounts of data with predictable query patterns.

Typically, a column-oriented database structure contains the following terms as shown in Table 5.3.

Table 5.3   Column-Oriented Database Structure

	Column Family A		Column Family B		
Row key 1	Col a	Col b	Col c	Col d	Col e
	Val 1a	Val 1b	Val 1c	Val 1d	Val 1e
	Timestamp	Timestamp	Timestamp	Timestamp	timestamp
Row key 2	Col a	Col b	Col c		Col f
	Val 2a	Val 2b	Val 2c		Val 2f
	Timestamp	Timestamp	Timestamp		timestamp

Table 5.4   Example of Column-Oriented Database

	Orders		*Customers*		
Row key 1	Order Id	Order value	Name	Email	Age
	1002	680/ Rs	Bob	bob@123. com	22
	Timestamp	Timestamp	Timestamp	Timestamp	timestamp
Row key 2	Order Id	Order value	Name		Contact
	2043	1285/ Rs	Alice		982345615
	Timestamp	Timestamp	Timestamp		timestamp

- Row: Each row contains a unique row identifier to identify the column data. Every row can have a different number of columns from other rows.
- Column: Each column is contained in its row. A column consists of a name value pair along with a timestamp of its creation date.
- Column family: A column family consists of multiple rows.

5.5 Document-Oriented Databases

Document-oriented databases are used to store semi-structured data and descriptions of that data in document format. A document-oriented database stores data in JavaScript Object Notation (JSON), Binary JavaScript Object Notation (BSON) or XML. JSON and BSON support the embedding of documents and arrays within other documents and arrays.

In a document-oriented database, documents can be nested and specific elements can be indexed for faster querying. Document-oriented databases are widespread among developers because they have the flexibility to restructure their

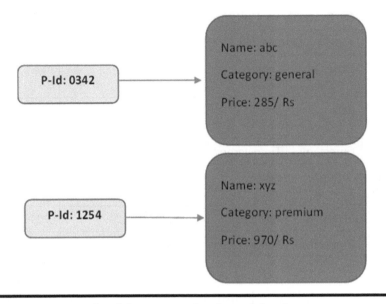

Figure 5.1   Example of documented-oriented database.

documents as per their business needs. This flexibility speeds development because, in effect, data becomes like code and is under the control of developers whereas, in SQL databases, to change the structure of a database, database administrators' intervention may be required. Figure 5.1 shows an example of a documented-oriented database.

5.6 Graph-Based Databases

A graph-based database uses graph structures to store data elements and to define the relationships between stored data elements. Graph databases are useful for identifying patterns in unstructured and semi-structured data content. Each data element to be stored is depicted as a node in the graph, and the connections that exist between it and other elements are represented as edges as shown in Figure 5.2. A unique identifier has been assigned to every node and edge in the network. A graph-oriented database is optimized to describe

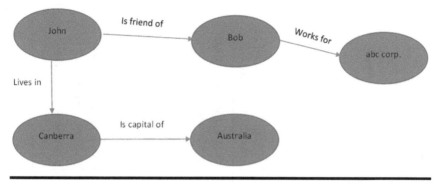

Figure 5.2   Graph-oriented data store.

and explore the connections between data elements, over-coming the overhead associated with joining multiple tables in SQL databases. Because graph-oriented databases store the relationships between data elements, they can support richer representations of data relationships. Also, graph-oriented data models can be augmented easily as they don't follow strict schemas unlike relational models.

5.7 Summary of NoSQL Databases

The NoSQL databases provide an efficient way of handling large volumes of unstructured data in a cloud or distributed environment. These databases don't follow strict schemas like relational databases and provide much flexibility to store data and analyze it as per the business needs. The NoSQL data-bases can be broadly classified into four types which are sum-marized in Table 5.5.

5.8 BASE Model of NoSQL

Although some of the NoSQL databases like Apache's CouchDB or IBM's Db2 follow traditional atomicity, consis-tency, isolation and durability (ACID) compliance at a certain

Table 5.5 Summary of Different Types of NoSQL Databases

Parameter	Key-Value Pair Based Databases	Column-Oriented Databases	Document-Oriented Databases	Graphs-Based Databases
Structure	Data is stored in a simple structure of a unique key and its associated value	Data is stored in tables where a row key can link to a large number of columns	Stores data in document-like structures which can be encoded in JASON-like formats	Data elements are stored as a node in a graph and the relations between different data elements are represented through edges of the graph
Use case	Session management, application logs, managing shopping carts, recording click stream data	Recommendation engines, catalogs, fraud detection, event-logging	Effective in content management and monitoring mobile and web applications, web analytics, e-commerce	Social media platforms, reservation systems or customer relationship management
Popular databases	Aerospike, DynamoDB, Redis, Riak	Accumulo, Amazon SimpleDB, Cassandra, HBase, Hypertable	Couchbase Server, CouchDB, MarkLogic, MongoDB	AllegroGraph, IBM Graph, Amazon Neptune, ArangoDB, Neo4j

level, most of the NoSQL databases are designed not to strictly follow the ACID rules and focus on availability even in the case of frequent failures.

5.8.1 CAP Theorem

In a distributed environment of NoSQL, it is not possible to provide high availability of data with consistency. The CAP theorem states that in a distributed environment with replications, at the same time one can get at most two of the three desired properties (consistency, availability and partition tolerance).

5.8.1.1 Consistency

Consistency assures that all of the different nodes have the same replicated copies of the data items. Consistency guarantees that every user should be able to view the most recent information regarding any data item whenever the status of a data item is changed.

5.8.1.2 Availability

Availability ensures that the database access is always available for every user and there is a good response time for different user queries. There shouldn't be any delay or break in activity.

5.8.1.3 Partition Tolerance

Partition tolerance means that the system can continue operating even if there is a network failure connecting the nodes which results in two or more partitions, where the nodes are disconnected from another part of the network and can only communicate with the other nodes within the partition. That means that the system continues to function and upholds its consistency guarantees despite network partitions. Since the database is partitioned, even if part of it is inaccessible, it will not have an impact on the other parts of the database. Partition tolerance provides graceful recovery from partitions once the partition heals.

5.8.2 BASE Model

Instead of the strict ACID model, to provide high availability, NoSQL databases build upon a softer model known as the **B**asically **A**vailable, **S**oft state, **E**ventual consistency (BASE) model (Chandra, 2015).

5.8.2.1 Basically Available

BASE-modeled NoSQL databases will ensure the availability of data by spreading and replicating it across the nodes of the database cluster. There will be a response to every user request even in case of network failure.

5.8.2.2 Soft State

NoSQL databases do not guarantee immediate consistency. Soft state indicates that the data values are not locked and can be changed over time by the user or the system.

5.8.2.3 Eventual Consistency

Eventual consistency denotes that the system will eventually reach a consistent state. Whenever there is a change made to a data item, it must be propagated to any other copies that exist in the system. Because certain copies of the data are updated all at once while others are updated over time, there is a possibility that the replication process will be delayed. The BASE model does not impose immediate consistency; there is a possibility that these replicas will differ in some ways, but in the end, they will all be equivalent to one another. The system will eventually become consistent once it stops receiving input.

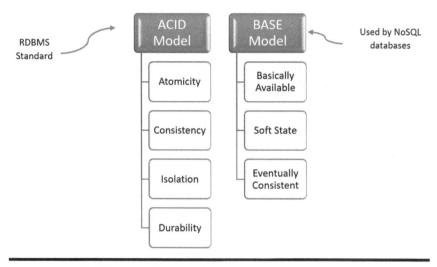

Figure 5.3   ACID vs BASE model.

5.8.3 ACID vs BASE Model

The traditional relational databases are strictly compliant with the ACID properties. In general, NoSQL databases focus on high availability and flexibility of handling large volumes of datasets and hence follow the BASE model. However, some of the NoSQL databases also follow ACID properties. The comparison between ACID and BASE models is summarized in Table 5.6.

5.9 Advantages of NoSQL

NoSQL databases manage large amounts of complex data in a way that is quick, diverse and scalable. The key benefits of NoSQL databases are that they:

- Facilitate flexible data model, capable of handling big data
- Simplify application development, particularly for interactive real-time applications
- Offer scalability for larger datasets

Table 5.6   Comparison of ACID Model and BASE Model

Parameter	ACID Model	BASE Model
Key feature	Highly consistent	Highly available
Simplicity	Simple	Complex
Data consistency	Strong	Weak
Scaling	Vertical	Horizontal
Implementation	Easy	Complex
Maintenance	High	Low
Example	Oracle, MySQL, SQL Server, graph-based NoSQL databases like Neo4j	MongoDB, Cassandra, Redis Amazon DynamoDB and Couchbase

- Are better suited for cloud, mobile, social media and big data requirements
- Lack a single failure point
- Are easy to replicate
- Allow for flexible schema design that may be modified without service delays or downtime

5.10 Disadvantages of NoSQL

Although NoSQL has gained a lot of popularity in recent times, it also has some challenges which need to be considered while implementing NoSQL databases.

- There are no norms for standardization.
- There are few capabilities for querying in NoSQL databases.
- NoSQL does not implement any of the conventional database properties, such as maintaining consistency even

when a large number of transactions are being processed all at once.
■ The lack of a firm database schema and constraints removes the data integrity safeguards that are built into relational and SQL database systems.

References

Chandra, D. G. (2015). BASE analysis of NoSQL database. *Future Generation Computer Systems, 52*, 13–21.

IBM Cloud Education. (2019, August). *NoSQL databases.* www.ibm .com. Retrieved from https://www.ibm.com/cloud/learn/nosql -databases

Chapter 6

Data Lakes

6.1 Introduction

The term "data lake" refers to a repository for vast amounts of unstructured data collected from diverse sources in a raw format. Whereas a traditional data warehouse organizes its data into hierarchical file systems, a data lake stores its information in a flat, object-oriented structure. In order to improve performance and facilitate data retrieval across regions, object storage saves data with metadata tags and a unique identifier (Jeavons, 2022). The data can be used by a wide variety of programs thanks to the data lake's use of low-cost object storage and open formats.

Data warehouses are expensive and proprietary, and they can't handle the modern use cases that most businesses want to address, but they do provide highly performant and scalable analytics to businesses. In order to overcome the drawbacks of traditional data warehouses, data lakes were created. Data lakes are used to store all of an organization's data in one place without first imposing a schema (i.e. a formal structure for how the data is organized), similar to how a data warehouse stores data. An organization's raw data can be ingested and stored in a data lake alongside its structured, tabular data sources (such as database tables) and intermediate data tables

 DOI: 10.1201/9781003441595-8

generated during the refinement process. Data lakes, in contrast to traditional databases and data warehouses, are capable of processing both structured and unstructured data, such as images, videos, audio files and documents, all of which are essential for modern machine learning and advanced analytics applications (Husain & Khanum, 2017).

6.2 Data Lake Architecture

Data lake architecture provides the seamless integration of structured and unstructured data from multiple sources across the organizations. The two main components of data lakes are storage and compute. Both storage and compute can be located either on-premises or in the cloud which provides flexibility in implementing data lakes based on organizational needs. Organizations can choose to stay completely on-premises, move the whole architecture to the cloud, consider multiple clouds or even can use a combination of cloud and on-premises locations.

Data lakes provide transformational capabilities to businesses in having the flexibility, agility and security of having a large volume of structured and unstructured historical as well as operational data readily available. The concept of zones is used to effectively implement a data lake. To keep the environment secure, organized and agile, these zones allow the logical and/or physical segregation of data. The number of zones depends on the implementation strategy, however generally we have three to four zones in a data lake.

A general data lake architecture has the following zones as shown in Figure 6.1 (Patel et al., 2017).

6.2.1 Transient Zone

Transient data like streaming pools and temporary copies are stored in the transient zone before being processed.

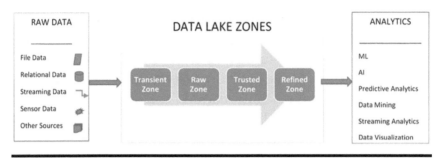

Figure 6.1 Data lake architecture with zones.

6.2.2 Raw Zone

In the raw zone, the data is preprocessed and secured before ingestion. The data goes through different operations in this zone like tokenization, encryption and other methods to make data secure and ready for processing.

6.2.3 Trusted Zone

The trusted zone holds the trusted data, which is preprocessed and validated for quality in the raw zone, for downstream systems.

6.2.4 Refined Zone

The processed and manipulated data, using external tools like Hive, is stored in the refined zone. This data is ready for transfer into the data lake for the application purpose.

6.3 Usage of Data Lakes

A data lake is used when the emphasis is on a flexible format storage for future use with no fixed storage, and limitations on file type. Data lakes use a flat architecture for data storage and facilitate quicker data retrieval with the help of metadata tags and identifiers. An increasingly vital aspect of modern data architectures is the ability to easily integrate new technologies, and data lakes are open format, allowing users to avoid lock-in to a proprietary system like a data warehouse. As a result of their scalability and use of object storage, data lakes are also extremely reliable and inexpensive. Organizations place a high value on advanced analytics and machine learning on unstructured data. Given these advantages, as well as the fact that a data lake can accept raw data in a wide variety of formats (structured, unstructured and semi-structured), it is evident that a data lake is the best option for storing data. When properly architected, data lakes enable the following.

6.3.1 Facilitating Data Science and Machine Learning Capabilities

Low-latency access to structured data for SQL analytics, data science and machine learning is made possible by data lakes. When storing data for later use in machine learning and analytics, keeping it in its raw form incurs very little cost and can be done indefinitely. Because data lakes provide the foundation for analytics and artificial intelligence, businesses across every industry are using them to increase revenue, save money and reduce risk.

6.3.2 Centralizing, Consolidating and Cataloguing Data

Data lakes provide a centralized and consolidated form of data storage, and with the catalogue feature, downstream users have a single location to go to find all sources of data, which solves the issues with data silos (such as data duplication, multiple security policies and difficulty with collaboration).

6.3.3 Seamless Integration of Diverse Data Sources and Formats

Data lakes facilitate the quick and seamless storage of data from diverse sources, batch and streaming data. Data lakes also support the seamless storage of data in various formats like video, images, binary files and more. The data is always current because the data lake serves as a repository for newly collected information.

6.3.4 Offering Various Self-Service Tools

Data lakes are incredibly flexible, enabling users with completely different skills, tools and languages to perform different analytics tasks all at once.

6.4 Data Lake Challenges

Despite their benefits, data lakes have failed to deliver on many of their promises because they are missing many key features, such as transaction support, data quality and governance enforcement and efficient performance optimizations.

6.4.1 Data Swamps

Inexperienced users can start dumping data into a data lake without a viable strategy or plan just like a messy dumping ground for data. It will become difficult to find the required data from these data swamps.

6.4.2 Slow Performance

Due to various issues like metadata management, the inefficient partitioning of data and other similar concerns, the performance of traditional query engines is slowed down as the amount of data in a data lake is increased.

6.4.3 Lack of Security Features

Due to limited access and the inability to delete or update data, data lakes are difficult to properly secure and govern. As a result of these constraints, compliance with regulatory requirements is extremely challenging. As a result, businesses often employ complex architectures, with data siloed away in various storage systems including data warehouses, databases and other systems across the enterprise, rather than relying solely on a traditional data lake to meet their needs.

6.4.4 Reliability Issues

Data lakes can have problems with data reliability without the right tools in place, making it hard for data scientists and analysts to reason with the data. Data corruption, problems with combining batch and streaming data and other factors can all contribute to these problems.

6.5 Data Lake Advantages and Disadvantages

The key advantages and disadvantages of using data lakes are summarized in Table 6.1.

6.6 Lake House

The lake house is an extension of the data lake that incorporates transactional storage to address the problems that come with the latter. A lake house is a data management

Table 6.1   Advantages and Disadvantages of Data Lakes

Advantages	Disadvantages
A data lake is an agile platform which enables multiple and advanced analytical methods to interpret the data.	Data storage and processing costs increase as data increases in the data lake.
"Schema on read" rather than "schema on write" provides more flexibility.	Often the data lake becomes a data swamp due to unstructured data and lack of incorporating metadata which makes it difficult to identify data useful for the application.
Supports easy integration of different types of data (structured, semi-structured and unstructured).	
Data analysis can be done later as per requirements.	Successfully mining the required data from a data lake requires a trained data scientist.
Raw data is always kept intact	
Data from the same source can be interpreted in different ways for different needs.	Inexperienced users can start dumping data into a data lake without a viable strategy or plan which leads to losing the track of data that's stored and makes it difficult to find the useful data when required.
Data lakes provide more scalability than traditional data warehouses.	

system that operates similarly to a data warehouse but directly on cloud data lakes. At the end of the day, a lake house makes it possible for traditional analytics, data science and machine learning to all coexist in one open framework (Armbrust, 2021).

Using a lake house, businesses can implement large-scale, cross-departmental projects in analytics, BI and machine learning, which can have a significant impact on their bottom line. Data engineers can create automated ETL pipelines, data scientists can join and enrich datasets to generate ever-more-accurate ML models, business intelligence analysts can create visual dashboards and reporting tools faster and easier than before, and data analysts can harvest rich insights by querying the data lake using SQL. All of these use cases can be executed in parallel on the data lake without the need to copy or move any of the data while new data is continuously being ingested.

6.6.1 Delta Lake

Delta Lake is an open format data management and governance layer that combines the best features of data lakes and data warehouses, making it the go-to choice for companies looking to construct a successful lake house. Delta Lake is used by businesses of all sizes and in a variety of sectors because it serves as a trustworthy, authoritative hub for teamwork. Delta Lake eliminates data silos and makes analytics available across the enterprise by providing quality, reliability, security and improved performance, for both streaming and batch operations. Delta Lake allows customers to construct a lake house that is both highly scalable and cost-effective, with features such as the elimination of data silos and the provision of self-serving analytics for end users.

6.7 Difference between Data Warehouses, Data Lakes and Lake Houses

The main differences between data warehouses, data lakes and lake houses are summarized in Table 6.2.

Table 6.2   Differences between Data Warehouses, Data Lakes and Lake Houses

Comparison Criteria	Data Warehouse	Data Lake	Lake House
Data type	Supports mainly structured data	Supports structured as well as semi-structured and unstructured data	Supports structured as well as semi-structured and unstructured data
Scalability	Easily scalable with low cost	Easily scalable with low cost	Scaling up is exponentially expensive
Type of users	Target users are data analysts	Target users are data scientists	Target users are data scientists, analysts and machine learning engineers
Format	Exclusive format	Open format	Open format
Reliability	Highly reliable	Low	Highly reliable
Complexity	Simple and easy access to data for reporting and analysis	Difficult to organize and explore large amounts of data without supporting tools	Simple structure like data warehouse but with more features like data lakes
Purpose	Specific purpose of data storage is defined	Data can be used for different purposes	Data can be used for different purposes
Storage	Processed data which is ready for use is stored	Raw data is stored for later analysis	Raw data is stored for later analysis
Performance	High	Poor	High
Cost	Comparatively very high	Low	low

6.8 Best Practices Regarding Data Lakes

The following are the best practices one should incorporate to get most of the benefits from a data lake (Patel et al., 2017).

6.8.1 Data Lake as Landing Zone

The data lake should be used as a landing zone to store all of your data, before any cleaning, transformation or aggregation operation. This data is used in the future for machine learning and data analysis.

6.8.2 Data Quality

For the effective performance of the system, the quality data should be maintained (Khan et al., 2015). A data lake supports all types of data; however different data sources require different quality control mechanisms. For example, to maintain the data quality data cleansing is an important step, but this will not much affect the result in the case of social media data analytics or data acquired from IoT devices. So we need to identify the correct quality measures that should be applied based on the application scenario.

6.8.3 Reliability

Due to the complexity of big data, it has been challenging to provide the same reliability and performance that databases have traditionally provided. Data lakes have been lacking these capabilities, but the incorporation of Delta Lake can improve the reliability and performance of the system.

6.8.4 Data Catalog

Use data catalog and metadata management tools at the point of ingestion to enable self-service data science and analytics.

Organizing data properly improves the ability to execute rapid queries on petabyte-scale datasets.

6.8.5 Security

Secure your data lake with role- and view-based access controls. More fine-grained tuning and control over the safety of your data lake is possible with the addition of view-based access control levels (ACLs) than with role-based controls alone (Verma et al., 2018).

6.8.6 Privacy

To ensure the privacy of the data, mask data containing private information before it enters the data lake. Pseudonymization is indeed a necessary step in GDPR compliance and long-term data storage.

6.8.7 Data Lineage

It is important to maintain a record of the relationships between the data coming into the data lake and the data existing in the data lake. These relations or data lineage help in identifying the changes happening in the datasets and the cause of the changes. Data lineage also helps to trace the origin of the data and how it moves in the data lake.

References

Armbrust, M., Ghodsi, A., Xin, R., & Zaharia, M. (2021). Lakehouse: A new generation of open platforms that unify DataWarehousing and advanced analytics. *Proceedings of the CIDR*. https://www.databricks.com: Retrieved from https://www.databricks.com/p/ebook/the-delta-lake-series-lakehouse

Husain, M. S., & Khanum, M. A.. (2017). Cloud computing in E-governance: Indian perspective. In Saleem Zoughbi (Ed.) *Securing government information and data in developing countries* (pp. 104–114). IGI.

Jeavons, D. (2022). *Introduction to data lakes*. www.databricks.com. Retrieved from https://www.databricks.com/discover/data-lakes/introduction

Khan, N., Husain, M. S., & Beg, M. R. (2015). Big data classification using evolutionary techniques: A survey. *IEEE International Conference on Engineering and Technology (ICETECH)* (pp. 243–247).

Patel, P., Wood, G., & Diaz, A.(2017, April 25). *Data lake governance best practices*. Retrieved from https://dzone.com: https://dzone.com/articles/data-lake-governance-best-practices

Verma, A., Arif, M., & Husain, M. S. (2018). Analysis of DDOS attack detection and prevention in cloud environment: A review. *International Journal of Advanced Research in Computer Science, 9*, 107–113.

Chapter 7

Deep Learning

7.1 Introduction

Machine learning typically focuses on representing the input data and then generalizing the learned patterns to be applied to new, previously unseen data. The quality of the data representation has a significant effect on how well machine learners perform on the data; bad data representations can hinder the effectiveness of even the most sophisticated and complex machine learners, while good data representations can propel the performance of even the most straightforward machine learners to new heights (Husain, 2020).

Feature engineering is a crucial part of machine learning because it involves building features and data representations from scratch. The majority of time and energy spent on a machine learning task goes toward feature engineering, which is typically highly domain-specific and requires substantial human input. A wide range of feature engineering algorithms have emerged which can be broadly categorized as wrapper methods, filter methods and embedded methods (Naveed, 2021). It would be a huge step forward for machine learning if feature engineering could be performed in a more automated and general manner, allowing practitioners to automatically

 DOI: 10.1201/9781003441595-9

extract such features without direct human input. Deep learning algorithms are one promising avenue of research into the automated extraction of complex data representations (features) at high levels of abstraction. Such algorithms develop a layered, hierarchical architecture of learning and representing data, where higher-level (more abstract) features are defined in terms of lower-level (less abstract) features. The hierarchical learning architecture of deep learning algorithms is motivated by artificial intelligence emulating the deep, layered learning process of the primary sensorial areas of the neocortex in the human brain, which automatically extracts features and abstractions from the underlying data (Arel et al., 2010).

Deep learning is a machine learning technique based on the traditional artificial neural network approach. However, instead of using single layer, in deep learning aka deep neural networks we have three or more hidden layers. These additional layers help to refine the model and optimize the predictions with large datasets.

Unlike traditional machine learning algorithms, where the laborious and complex task of feature selection is done by humans, deep learning automatically performs the feature selection from the datasets. Deep learning simulates the behavior of the human brain for learning and produces fast and accurate results.

7.2 Deep Learning Architecture

The artificial neural network (ANN) is the basic architecture behind deep learning. Various architectures and algorithms have been proposed like convolutional neural networks (CNN) and long short-term memory (LSTM). With the advent of graphical processing units (GPUs) and the availability of huge volumes of data, i.e. big data, for training, deep learning is now at the forefront of data analysis and is producing effective results in a broad spectrum of domains.

As shown in Figure 7.1 (Madhavan & Jones, 2017), deep learning architectures can be broadly classified as supervised learning architecture and unsupervised learning architecture.

7.2.1 Supervised Learning

In supervised learning mode, the model uses a labeled dataset for training purposes. The most common types of supervised learning architecture for deep learning are convolutional neural networks (CNN) and recurrent neural networks (RNN).

7.2.1.1 Convolutional Neural Networks (CNN)

Convolutional neural network architecture uses 2D convolutional layers and is more suitable for 2D data such as images. In CNN we can have n numbers of hidden layers, where the initial layers are used for feature extraction and the later layers are used to optimize the results by combining these extracted features into high level attributes. CNNs are very effective in applications like image recognition, video analysis and natural language processing.

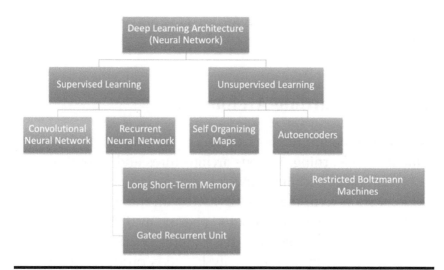

Figure 7.1   Deep learning architectures (Samaya Madhavan, 2017).

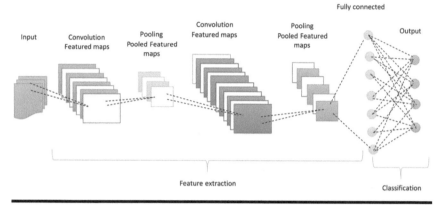

Figure 7.2   Convolutional neural network architecture.

Apart from the input and output layers, CNN architecture is comprised of three types of layers as shown in Figure 7.2: the convolutional layer, pooling layer and fully connected layer (O'Shea & Nash, 2015).

■ **Convolutional layer**: In convolutional layers, a mathematical convolutional operation is applied to extract features of the input (generally an image). The rectified linear unit (ReLu) is implemented to apply an "element-wise" activation function to the output of the activation produced by the previous layer. The result of the convolution operation termed the "feature map" is passed to the next layer.

■ **Pooling layer**: The pooling layer performs down sampling along the spatial dimensionality of the given input, further reducing the number of parameters within that activation to reduce the computational cost. Basically this layer summarizes the features generated by a convolution layer. There are different approaches like max pooling, average pooling and sum pooling which can be implanted in this layer.

■ **Fully connected layer**: The fully connected layer uses the output from the convolution process and applies

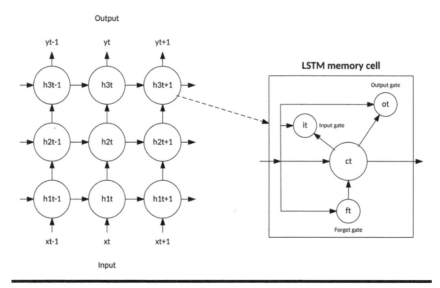

Figure 7.3a LSTM architecture (Samaya Madhavan, 2017).

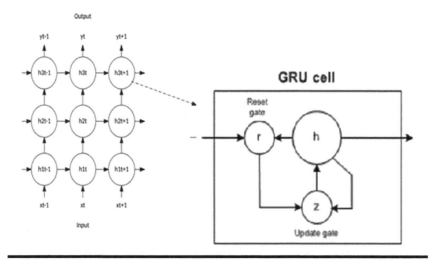

Figure 7.3b GRU architecture (Samaya Madhavan, 2017).

mathematical operations using weights and biases to pro-
duce class scores to be used for classification purposes.
 – At times, when all the features are connected to the
   FC layer, it may cause the issue of **overfitting**. To

deal with the problem of overfitting a **dropout** layer is used, where randomly around 30% of the neurons are dropped out of the neural network.

7.2.1.2 Recurrent Neural Networks (RNN)

An RNN is a variant of a feed forward neural network in which the output of a particular layer is stored and fed back to the input in order to predict the output of the layer. RNNs are very effective in the case of ordinal or temporal problems where they take sequential or time series data and precisely predict the next output by using the previous output stored in the hidden layer as an input for the current step. The main application areas of RNN are language translation, music generation, sentiment analysis, speech recognition, name entity recognition, image captioning and time series forecasting, etc. There are different variants of traditional RNN architecture like long short-term memory (LSTM), bidirectional recurrent neural networks (BRNN) and gated recurrent units (GRUs).

- **Long short-term memory (LSTM)**: LSTM is based on the concept of a memory cell in the hidden layers of the neural network. This cell retains its value for a short or long time as a function of its inputs, and allows the system to remember what's important and not just its last computed value. These memory cells have three gates – an input gate, an output gate and a forget gate. These gates control the flow of information which is needed to predict the output in the network.
- **Gated recurrent units (GRUs)**: Instead of three gates like LSTM, the GRU has two gates, namely the update gate and reset gate, to control how much and which information to retain. This model makes GRU simpler, faster and more efficient than LSTM; however it is less expressive than LSTM.

- **Bidirectional recurrent neural networks (BRNN)**:
  Unlike the traditional RNN which uses the previous output to predict the outcome of the current state, the bidirectional RNN also take the future data in predicting the outcome. BRNN provides more accurate results than traditional RNN models.

7.2.2 *Unsupervised Learning*

In unsupervised learning mode, the model doesn't have any labeled dataset for training purposes. The most common types of unsupervised learning architecture for deep learning are self-organized maps, autoencoders, restricted Boltzmann machines, deep belief networks and deep stacking networks.

7.2.2.1 *Self-Organized Maps*

The self-organized map (SOM), invented by Teuvo Kohonen (also called the Kohonen map), is an unsupervised artificial neural network. SOM does not use the activation function for training; instead it uses a competitive learning algorithm to train its network. SOM has only two layers, an input layer and an output layer, as shown in Figure 7.4. Initially a random

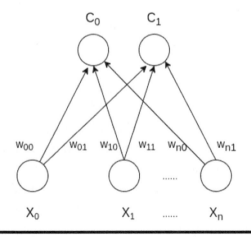

Figure 7.4   SOM architecture (with two clusters and n input features).

weight is initialized for each feature of the input set and a weight-vector is assigned to each neuron in SOM. The distances (generally Euclidean distance) between the neurons of the output layer and these weight-vectors are measured, and the vector node with the lowest distance will be considered to be the most accurate representation of the input and is marked as the best matching unit (BMU). The neighboring nodes (based on the distance) along with the winner vector form a cluster. The weights of the nodes in the clusters are updated proportionally to the distance. SOM is very effective in applications like dimensionality reduction, clustering high-dimensional inputs to two-dimensional output, radiant grade result and cluster visualization.

7.2.2.2 Autoencoders

Autoencoders are a variation of artificial neural networks with three layers as shown in Figure 7.5. The hidden layer has a smaller number of nodes compared to the input layer. An

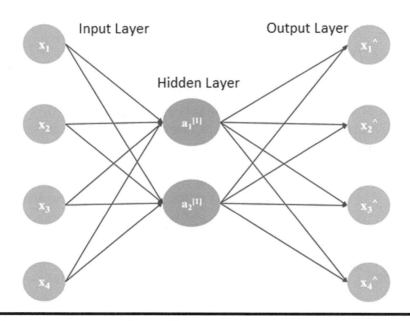

Figure 7.5   Autoencoder architecture.

encoding scheme is used to encode the input layer into the hidden layer. Hence, the hidden layer represents a compressed form of the actual input. The model is then trained to get the output from the hidden layer using a decoding scheme. Autoencoders are "self-supervised" models where the output is compared with the original input and the error is back propagated to adjust the weights. Autoencoders are used for data compression/decompression, dimensionality reduction and data interpolation.

7.2.2.3 Restricted Boltzmann Machines (RBM)

A restricted Boltzmann machine (RBM) is an artificial neural network with two layers: an input layer and hidden layers as shown in Figure 7.6. RBM measures the probability distribution of the training set just like a traditional Boltzmann machine to predict unseen data. In RBMs every node in a hidden layer is connected to every node in a visible layer; however, it restricts the connection of nodes within a layer unlike a traditional Boltzmann machine. RBMs are used for dimensionality reduction, classification, regression and collaborative filtering.

7.2.2.4 Deep Belief Networks (DBN)

A deep belief network is a typical network architecture composed of multiple layers of RBMs as shown in Figure 7.7. The raw data is provided to the input layer, and then the output of one RBM works as the input for the next hidden layer

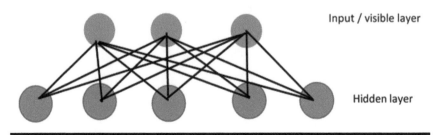

Figure 7.6   Restricted Boltzmann machine architecture.

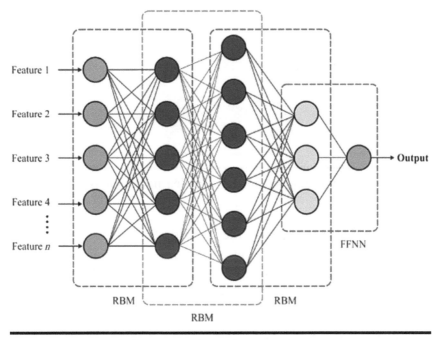

Figure 7.7   Deep belief network architecture.

consecutively until we get the optimized result. DBNs are effectively used in applications like image recognition, information retrieval, video sequences, motion capture data, natural language understanding and failure prediction.

7.3 Training Approaches for Deep Learning Models

There are different ways one can implement and train a deep learning model. The three common approaches for implementing a deep learning model are shown in Figure 7.8.

7.3.1 Training from Scratch

Typically for new applications, a deep network is designed from scratch and trained using a very large labeled dataset to

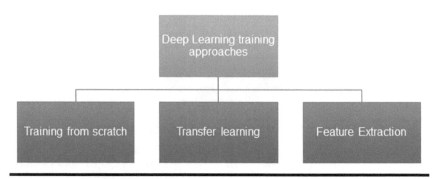

Figure 7.8   Training approaches for deep learning models.

extract the features and provide learning to the model. These networks typically take a long time (days or weeks) to train because of the large amount of data used and the high rate of learning and are thus less common.

7.3.2 Transfer Learning

Transfer learning is the most common approach to train a deep learning model. In transfer learning, a pre-trained model like GoogLeNet or AlexNet is used and fine-tuned (modified/ enhanced) using new data containing previously unknown classes. The training is comparatively faster and needs only a few adjustments to perform the effective classification of new data. Transfer learning also has the advantage of needing much less data for training, so the computation time drops to minutes or hours.

7.3.3 Feature Extraction

This is a more specialized approach to deep learning. As different layers in a deep learning model are used to learn certain features from the datasets, the network can be used as a feature extractor. These features can be extracted from the network during the training phase and can be used as input to any machine learning model.

7.4 Challenges in Deep Learning Implementation

Deep learning has gained immense popularity in recent years; however, it does come with its own set of challenges that the research community is working hard to resolve. The three major challenges in the effective implementation of deep learning are as follows.

7.4.1 Data Volume Required

Effective deep learning model implementation requires high volumes of data for training. Having this much data is not always easy. Additionally, while we can have large amounts of data on some topic, many times it is not labeled so we cannot use it to train any kind of supervised learning algorithm. To acquire this huge amount of data and perform cleaning and labeling operations to make sure that it is ready for your deep learning model is a time-consuming process and requires tremendous data processing capabilities. Thus providing great performance with much less training data is one of the main challenges of deep learning.

7.4.2 Biasness

Another challenge in implementing deep learning is the underlying bias in the data itself. Biased data can lead to poor performance of the deep learning model. Before feeding the data to the deep learning model, debiasing of the data is strongly recommended; also there is a strong need to allow models to learn in a balanced fashion.

7.4.3 Explainability

Deep learning algorithms have been proven to beat human-level accuracy; however, they lack explainability. There is no clear way to backtrack and provide the reasoning behind each prediction made by the model. This makes it difficult to use in applications such as finance where there are directives to provide the reasoning behind every financial transaction like the approval or rejection of a credit card for a particular user.

7.5 Applications of Deep Learning

In recent years, deep learning has emerged as a trend and is being used in various domains. Some of the key applications of deep learning are discussed below.

7.5.1 Healthcare Industry

Nowadays, various healthcare organizations have switched to the digitization of records and medical images to exclude any human error and operate smoothly. With easier access to accelerated GPU and the availability of huge amounts of electronic data, deep learning technology has had a very important effect on the healthcare industry.

Using image recognition, cancer detection from MRI imaging and X-rays has been surpassing human levels of accuracy with much shorter processing times.

7.5.2 Autonomous Vehicles

In spite of being a risky field of automation, self-driving cars have recently taken a turn towards becoming a reality. Deep learning-based models are trained and tried under simulated environments to automatically detect objects such as stop signs, traffic lights and pedestrians on the road and the results are quite encouraging.

7.5.3 E-Commerce

More personalized and accurate recommendations enable the users to view all of the options that they can choose from and easily shop for the items they are looking for. Personalized recommendations also accelerate sales and, thus, benefit sellers. Deep learning models are very effective in the personalized recommendation of products.

7.5.4 Personal Assistant

Personal assistants like Siri, Alexa and Google Assistant are very popular nowadays. These smart assistants use deep learning models for different tasks such as personalized voice recognition, personalized recommendations and text generation.

7.5.5 Medical Research

Deep learning models are used by cancer researchers at UCLA to automatically detect cancer cells. Genomics, drug discovery and clinical trial matching are other popular medical research applications of deep learning.

7.5.6 Customer Service

Straightforward forms of artificial intelligence and machine learning methods like chatbots have already established their effectiveness in improving customer service tasks. With the application of deep learning technology sophisticated chatbot solutions can be developed. These advanced chatbots will be able to provide multiple answers based on the user's history and even provide answers to ambiguous questions.

7.5.7 Finance Industry

Predictive analytics using deep learning models in financial institutions has led to a series of benefits that might not have been possible otherwise. These models are very helpful in the assessment of business risks, fraud detection, assessment for loan/credit card approval and stock market analysis.

7.5.8 Industrial Automation

Industries are using deep learning methods for product quality control and predicting the risk factors or life of components used in the industry. Deep learning models also help in improving worker safety around heavy machinery by automatically detecting when people or objects are within an unsafe distance of machines.

7.5.9 Smart Devices

Deep learning is being used in various smart devices to assist people with accessibility needs like automated hearing and speech translation, for example, home assistance devices.

7.5.10 Aerospace and Defense

Deep learning is used to identify objects from satellites that locate areas of interest, and identify safe or unsafe zones for troops.

7.5.11 Weather Predictions

Last but not least, deep learning models are also very helpful in weather predictions.

References

Arel, I., Rose, D. C., & Karnowski, T. P.(2010). Deep machine learning - A new frontier in artificial intelligence research [research frontier]. *IEEE Computational Intelligence Magazine* (pp. 13–18).

Husain, M. S. (2020). Critical concepts and techniques for information retrieval system. In Brojo Kishore Mishra, Raghvendra Kumar (Eds.) *Natural language processing in artificial intelligence* (pp. 29–51). Apple Academic Press.

Madhavan, S., & Jones, M. T. (2017). *Deep learning architectures.* https://developer.ibm.com: https://developer.ibm.com/articles/cc -machine-learning-deep-learning-architectures/

Naveed, N., Madhloom, H. T., & Husain, M. S. (2021). Breast cancer diagnosis using wrapper-based feature selection and artificial neural network. *Applied Computer Science.* Vol. 17, no. 3 pp. 19–30

O'Shea, K., & Nash, R.(2015). An introduction to convolutional neural networks. *Neural and Evolutionary Computing.* ArXiv, abs/1511.08458.

Chapter 8

Blockchain

8.1 Introduction

A blockchain is a decentralized, distributed digital ledger based on cryptographic hash functions that are used to record transactions across many computers. Blockchain maintains a continuously growing list of ordered records, called "blocks." These blocks are linked using cryptography to form a chain. Each block contains a cryptographic hash of the previous block, a timestamp and transaction data. It is considered to be impossible to change, hack or manipulate the information recorded on these ledgers.

The purpose of the blockchain is to share information amongst all parties that access it via an application in a protected manner, meaning that any alteration is easily and immediately detectable.

8.2 Structure of the Blockchain

The blockchain stores transaction records in blocks linked together in sequence to form a chain. Each block contains a hash, timestamped batches of recent valid transactions and the

 DOI: 10.1201/9781003441595-10

hash of the previous block. The previous block hash links the blocks together and prevents any block from being altered or a block being inserted between two existing blocks. A block is composed of a header containing all the metadata and a body including all transaction details as shown in Figure 8.1. A blockchain starts from its genesis block and new blocks are appended periodically as shown in Figure 8.2.

The parent block hash is a part of the metadata that links the current block to the one before it in the blockchain. Metadata also contains information about the mining like the difficulty level and timestamps. The nonce is a string of random numbers that is attached to the hashed contents of the block, which is then rehashed. The Merkle tree root is a data structure that is included in the final metadata. This data structure is used to efficiently summarize all of the transaction details that are contained within the associated block.

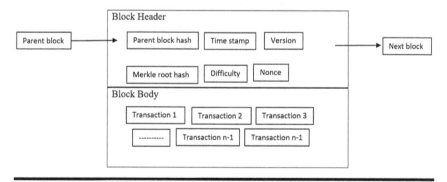

Figure 8.1   Structure of a block.

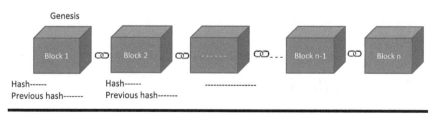

Figure 8.2   Structure of blockchain.

8.3 Security Features of the Blockchain

Blocks in a blockchain contain two types of information. The first is the payload which is application-specific information that records transactions or smart contracts, and the second is internal information that secures the block and specifies how it's chained to another. Security in blockchains is implemented at two levels.

8.3.1 Block Linking

For every new block, a hash is generated using the hash of the parent block and a random number "nonce." Since the nonce is hard to calculate, misplacing a block or changing the content of a block means redoing nonce computations of all blocks subsequently linked to it which is infeasible.

8.3.2 Consensus Mechanism

A blockchain system functions in a peer-to-peer mode without a central trusted entity. The consensus mechanism is based on verification by every node that the received information complies with a set of predefined rules, and on verification of the nonce. For consensus, a majority of nodes (over 51%) need to agree on the next block that extends the chain.

8.4 Types of Blockchain

There are four different types of blockchain as shown in Figure 8.3.

8.4.1 Public Blockchain

The public blockchain is the most simple and easily accessible blockchain for the general public. Any agent can sign into

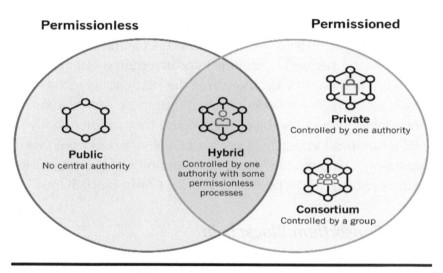

Figure 8.3   Types of blockchain (Wegrzyn & Wang, 2021).

a public blockchain and become an authorized participant, which allows them to become a user, miner or developer. Public blockchains are open-source, decentralized and fully distributed networks. Public blockchains do not impose any restrictions and do not require permission to use. Every node has unrestricted access to the ledger, which ensures that all transactions can be viewed by all parties. The key advantage of public blockchains is that they don't have a central control. To ensure the integrity of the public blockchain, each and every node participates in the various consensus procedures. Examples of public blockchains are mining activities and the trading of cryptocurrencies like Bitcoin, Ethereum and Litecoin.

8.4.2 *Private Blockchain*

A private blockchain is limited, centralized, permissioned and can only operate within closed networks. Each private blockchain has a centralized authority that has complete control over the accessibility, participation and permission of the blockchain network. To join a private blockchain network, permission is required from the centralized authority. The ledger is accessible only to the authorized users, and the authorization of the network's administrator is required before any alteration, additions or deletions may be made to its records. Private blockchain networks are therefore more secure and controllable than public blockchains, and they are frequently used in applications such as private businesses, electronic voting, supply chain management, etc. Examples of private blockchain networks are Hyperledger and R3 Corda blockchains.

8.4.3 Consortium Blockchain

The consortium blockchain is a subclass of private blockchain that differs from other types of private blockchain in that instead of just one, multiple organizations control and maintain the blockchain. As a result, it offers advantages that are analogous to those of a private blockchain. A consortium blockchain offers better security. Additionally, consortium blockchains are optimal for collaboration with multiple organizations. Consortium blockchains are most frequently utilized by financial institutions, governmental organizations and other types of collaborative institutes. Examples of consortium blockchains are the Energy Web Foundation and R3.

8.4.4 Hybrid Blockchain

Combinations of public and private blockchains are known as hybrid blockchains. Hybrid blockchain networks are private blockchains that allow special access for authorized individuals. They combine the privacy and permissioned features of private blockchains with the ease-of-use, flexibility and transparency of public blockchains on a single platform. Dragonchain is the most common example of a hybrid blockchain.

The comparison of the three types of blockchains is summarized in the Table 8.1.

Table 8.1 Types of Blockchains

Parameter	Public	Private	Consortium
Authority	No central authority	Single central authority	Multiple central authority
Participants	Anybody	Allowed agents	Allowed agents
Permission	No permission required	Permissioned	Permissioned
Decentralization	Fully decentralized	Centralized	Less centralized
Reading rights	Anyone	Invited user	Case dependent
Writing rights	Anyone	Approved user	Approved user
Consensus	PoS/PoW	Multiparty consensus	Multiparty consensus
Speed	Slow	Fast	Fast
Usability	Document validations and IoT operations	Supply chain, real estate and asset ownership	Finance, supply chain and research work

8.5 Blockchain Evolution

The theoretical concept of allotting a timestamp to a digital document using an encrypted chain that can verify when data was created as well as identify any changes made was proposed by Stuart Haber and W. Scott Stornetta in 1991. However, the actual implementation of this concept into technology was first done by Satoshi Nakamoto, a pseudonym behind an individual/organization, in 2008. Satoshi Nakamoto

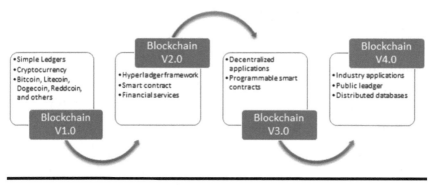

Figure 8.4   Evolution of blockchain.

used this concept to develop the first cryptocurrency, "Bitcoin." Since then blockchains have evolved with time as shown in Figure 8.4.

8.5.1 The First Generation (Blockchain 1.0: Cryptocurrency)

The first generation of blockchains aimed to design a decentralized monetary platform that puts the control back in the hands of the users. This technology enables peer-to-peer monetary transactions without any centralized control like a bank or financial institution and hence improves the financial systems in place. The first generation blockchain has limited functionality; however, the developers realized that this technology holds immense potential.

8.5.2 The Second Generation (Blockchain 2.0: Smart Contracts)

The second generation of blockchains aims at designing a digital ecosystem that not only facilitates peer-to-peer transactions but also adds a layer of "terms and conditions" so that people can agree on terms in smart contracts rather than relying on intermediaries.

Table 8.2 Comparison of Blockchain Generations

Parameter	Blockchain 1.0	Blockchain 2.0	Blockchain 3.0	Blockchain 4.0
Underlying concept	Distributed ledger technology (DLT)	Smart contracts	Decentralized apps	Blockchain with AI
Consensus mechanism	Proof of work (PoW)	Delegated proof of work	Proof of stake (PoS), proof of authority (PoA)	Proof of integrity (PoI)
Scalability	Not scalable	Not scalable	Scalable	Highly scalable
Interoperability	No	No	Supported	Highly interoperable
Verification	By miners	Using smart contracts	Verification mechanism inbuilt in dApps	Automated verification
Speed	7 TPS	15 TPS	1000s of TPS	M TPS
Energy consumption	High	Moderate	Energy efficient	Highly energy efficient
Examples	Bitcoin, Litecoin, Dogecoin, Reddcoin	Ethereum, BAT	Ethereum 2.0, Polkadot, Cardano, Nano, IOTA, COTI	Holochain, Qurakchain, Matrix AI, DeepBrain Chain, MetaMUI and SingularityNet
Applications	Financial sector	Decentralized finance (DeFi), web browsing, gaming, identity management, supply chain management	Industries like finance, government and retail	Industry 4.0

8.5.3 The Third Generation (Blockchain 3.0: DApps)

The third generation blockchains aim to resolve fundamental flaws that existed in the previous two generations including scalability and interoperability. Blockchain 3.0 provides more scalability which means it can tolerate mass adoption without suffering from issues like slow transaction times and closed systems. Interoperability is crucial as businesses rely on collaboration and information sharing across platforms. Blockchain 3.0 supports cross-chain transactions.

8.5.4 The Fourth Generation (Blockchain 4.0: Industry Applications)

The fourth generation of blockchain aims to contribute to the industry 4.0 revolution by providing an increased degree of scalability, privacy and security insurance. Various industries like supply chain management, healthcare and asset management are adopting blockchain technology to significantly improve their performance.

8.6 Advantages of Blockchain

Blockchain is an emerging technology with many advantages in an increasingly digital world:

■ **Highly secure**: Blockchain's security features protect against tampering, fraud and cybercrime. Blockchain supports immutability, meaning it is impossible to erase or replace recorded data. It uses a digital signature feature to conduct fraud-free transactions, making it impossible for other users to corrupt or change the data of an individual without a specific digital signature.

- **Transparency**: Blockchain is decentralized, meaning any network member can verify data recorded in the blockchain. Therefore, the public can trust the network.
- **Smoother and faster transactions**: Conventionally, the user needs the approval of regulatory authorities like a government or bank for transactions; however, with blockchain, transactions are done with the mutual consensus of users resulting in smoother and faster transactions.
- **Censorship**: Blockchain technology is free from censorship since it is not under the control of any single party. Therefore, no single authority can interrupt the operation of the network.
- **Automation capability**: Blockchain is programmable and can generate systematic actions, events and payments automatically. With the use of smart contracts, human interference can be reduced and the next step in the transaction or process is automatically triggered when the criteria of the trigger are met.
- **Traceability**: Blockchain creates an irreversible audit trail, allowing easy tracing of changes in any block on the network.
- **Time saving**: Traditional transaction processes require third-party mediation and are time-consuming. Blockchain slashes transaction times from days to minutes. Transaction settlement is faster because it doesn't require verification by a central authority.
- **Cost saving**: Transactions need less oversight. Participants can exchange items of value directly. Blockchain eliminates duplication of effort because participants have access to a shared ledger.

8.7 Disadvantages of Blockchain

Blockchain is the current trend and many organizations and individuals are looking forward to making best use of it.

However, there are some key disadvantages of blockchain which should not be ignored (Budhi, 2022)

8.7.1 Security Risk

Blockchain involves cryptography for integrity and security with the use of public and private keys. If a user loses their private key, they may face various security issues.

8.7.2 Speed and Performance

Blockchain technology carries out multiple operations to perform one transaction. These operations include signature verification, a consensus mechanism and implementing redundancy, where the network requires each node to play a crucial role in verifying and storing each transaction. Because of these computations blockchain is considerably slower than a traditional database.

8.7.3 Scalability

Scalability restrictions are another disadvantage of blockchain networks. The number of transactions per node is limited in blockchain. Hence, it may take a lot of time to complete multiple transactions.

8.7.4 Data Modification

In blockchain, it is not possible to change or add information after it is recorded. To alter any information requires rewriting the codes in all of the blocks, which is time-consuming and expensive. The downside of this feature is that it is hard to correct a mistake or make any necessary adjustments.

8.7.5 High Implementation Cost

Compared to a traditional database, blockchain implementation is costlier and needs proper planning and execution.

8.8 Applications of Blockchain

While blockchain is still largely confined to use in recording and storing transactions for cryptocurrencies, there are various industries that are implementing blockchain for different applications. Key application aspects of blockchain technologies are:

- Virtual coins
- Smart contracts
- Money transfer and payment processing
- Digital IDs
- Secure data sharing
- Royalty and copyright protection
- Secure data backup

8.8.1 Banking and Financial Industry

Blockchain technology helps in increasing operational efficiencies across the banking and financial industries, including global trade, trade finance, clearing and settlement, consumer banking, lending and other transactions.

8.8.2 Healthcare industry

Blockchain technology helps the healthcare industry to improve security for patient's private data while making it easier to share records across stakeholders like patients, doctors, healthcare agencies and researchers. Blockchain enables patients to have complete control over their data access which increases trust in the system.

8.8.3 Supply Chain Management

By providing end-to-end transparency, streamlining processes and resolving issues faster blockchain helps in building trust between trading partners and improving supply chain management.

8.8.4 Food Chain Management

Blockchain technology can be effectively used in the food industry to ensure food safety and freshness and reduce waste. In the event of contamination, food can be traced back to its source in seconds rather than days.

8.8.5 Governance

Blockchain technology can be used for smart governance. The secure sharing of data between citizens and agencies can increase trust in the government while providing an immutable audit trail for regulatory compliance, contract management, identity management and citizen services. Blockchain technology-enabled digital voting provides enough transparency so that any regulators can see if something was altered on the network.

8.8.6 Internet of Things Network Management

Blockchain technology can be very effective in regulating IoT networks to identify devices connected to a wireless network, monitor the activity of those devices and determine how trustworthy those devices are. It can also be used to automatically measure the trustworthiness of new devices being added to the network, such as cars and smartphones.

References

Budhi, V. (2022). *Advantages and disadvantages of blockchain technology*. Retrieved from https://www.forbes.com/sites/for-bestechcouncil/2022/10/20/advantages-and-disadvantages-of -blockchain-technology/?sh=45ea42ef3453

Wegrzyn, K. E., & Wang, E. (2021). *Types of blockchain: Public, private, or something in between*. Retrieved from https://www.foley .com: https://www.foley.com/en/insights/publications/2021/08/ types-of-blockchain-public-private-between

BIG DATA APPLICATIONS

Chapter 9

Big Data for Healthcare

9.1 Introduction

The exponential growth in digitized healthcare data has opened a significant avenue for big data analytics in improving and optimizing healthcare services. The healthcare industries have generated an enormous amount of healthcare data over the past couple of years. These healthcare data generally incorporate electronic health records (EHRs) such as patients' medical history, physician notes, clinical reports, biometric data and other medical data related to health. Advanced technologies like sensor systems, cameras, wearable devices and smartphones also contribute in acquiring important healthcare data.

9.2 Benefits of Big Data Analytics in Healthcare

With proper planning and implementation big data analytics can be very effective in improving the healthcare industry. Big data analytics is being used in different aspects of healthcare like **early diagnosis**, big data visualization in cardiology (Nazir, 2019), breast cancer diagnosis (Naveed, 2021), diabetes prediction (Philip, 2022), identifying mental stress or illness (Husain, 2019; PhilipTariq, 2019; Khan, 2018), the detection of

DOI: 10.1201/9781003441595-12

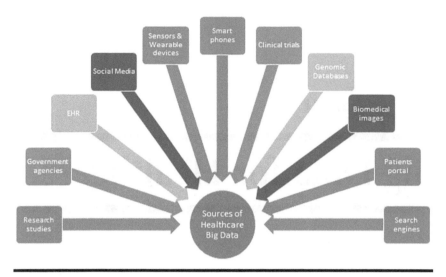

Figure 9.1   Key sources of healthcare big data.

abnormal behavior (Zhou et al., 2020), **real-time healthcare monitoring** (Bhatt & Chakraborty, 2021), **pervasive healthcare** (Husain et al., 2022; Li, 2020; Hirata, 2020; Jindal et al., 2018; Hooda et al., 2021), **clinical research** (Yu et al., 2019), **healthcare recommendation systems** (Lambay, 2020), **telemedicine** (Galletta et al., 2019) and **security and privacy** (Chakraborty et al., 2019; Ghayvat et al., 2022; Bi, 2022; Jayanthilladevi et al., 2020; Tripathi, 2021).

In general big data analytics can effectively contribute to enhanced patient care, decision making and healthcare planning, identifying best practices and effective treatments (Raja et al., 2020). Some of the specific benefits of big data analytics can be summarized as shown in Figure 9.2.

9.2.1 Improved Healthcare

Big data analytics enables medical professionals to cure diseases, predict epidemics, reduce medical errors, avoid preventable deaths and improve quality of life. Big data analytics is also very useful in preventing the duplication of treatment and unnecessary laboratory tests by instantly accessing and

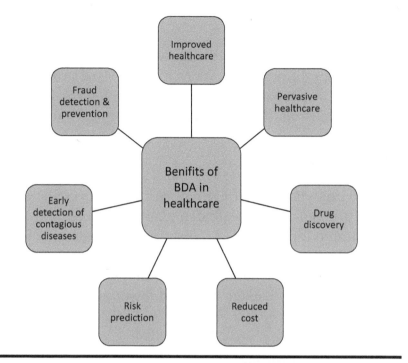

Figure 9.2   Benefits of big data analytics in healthcare.

tracking the patient's medical history to determine the patient's condition progress. This on-time coordination of the patient's records can be used to increase the effectiveness and efficiency of care delivery.

9.2.2 *Pervasive Healthcare*

Big data analytics has transformed patient care by identifying infections swiftly and suggesting the right treatments to patients. With the help of the latest advancements in electronic devices like the Fitbit activity tracker and the Apple Watch big data analytics has revolutionized personalized care for specific patients and provides better 24/7 medical care. This can be helpful in monitoring the physical activity levels of patients and effectively managing their health such as medication adherence, diet, exercise, etc., irrespective of their locations.

9.2.3 Drug Discovery

Pharmaceutical industries are effectively making use of big data analytics for drug discoveries to help physicians, pharmaceutical developers and other healthcare professionals in getting the right drug to the right patient at the right time.

9.2.4 Reduced Cost

Big data analytics effectively reduces the costs of the processing and storing of healthcare data and then applies sophisticated techniques to transform this huge volume of data into valuable outcomes. Big data analytics also provides greater insight about individual cases which results in shorter hospital stays and fewer admissions and re-admissions.

9.2.5 Risk Prediction

By using predictive analytics, the users with more risk can be identified early and can be treated well in time, not only saving money and time but also saving lives.

9.2.6 Early Detection of the Spread of Diseases

Big data analytics can be very effective in predicting the outbreak of contagious diseases like COVID-19 and preventive mechanisms can be incorporated in time.

9.2.7 Fraud Detection and Prevention

One of the key applications of big data analytics in the healthcare sector is fraud detection and prevention. Sophisticated data mining and machine learning techniques have been proved to be very effective for fraud detection in healthcare.

9.2.8 Clinical Operations

Big data analytics helps in determining specific methods of diagnosing patients and providing precise, clinically important and cost-effective treatment to patients.

9.3 Challenges in Implementing Big Data in Healthcare

Healthcare organizations face challenges with healthcare data that fall into several major categories as shown in Figure 9.3.

9.3.1 Confidentiality and Data Security

Personal data is critical for any individual, and ensuring privacy is of very high importance especially in the case of patients' data. Inefficient measures of privacy for medical

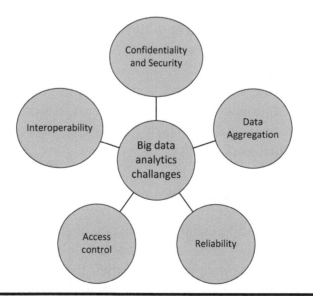

Figure 9.3   Challenges of big data analytics in healthcare (Imran, 2021).

and scientific data may result in public data which can be accessed openly. On the other hand for effective data analytics more and more relevant data is required which is hard to get because of security and privacy issues.

9.3.2 Data Aggregation

There are multiple sources which generate the healthcare data required for analytics as shown in Figure 9.1. Acquiring data from multiple heterogeneous sources is a complex task. It required good knowledge about the data sources to identify the correct source relevant to the application. Moreover, the data acquired from these sources is in different formats so a lot of preprocessing operations need to be implemented to make the data ready for analytics.

9.3.3 Reliability

Ensuring the reliability of data in big data analytics for health-care is another big challenge, as data is acquired from multiple heterogeneous sources and is in different formats. If the data is not properly cleaned and normalized before the analytics it may lead to wrong results.

Also, there are various tools and techniques for big data analytics; inexperienced staff can choose an inappropriate approach for their analysis which can lead to reduced accuracy and sub-optimal performance.

9.3.4 Access Control

To ensure the confidentiality and privacy of patients' records we need to manage access control so that only authorized users can access the data relevant to their functional areas. Granular access control enables patients' and medical profes-sionals' responsibilities, privileges, rights and roles to be set such that users related to the hospital are given privileges only to their relevant data or functional area of the system.

9.3.5 Interoperability

In the presence of multiple components and their different users in the healthcare system, interoperability between different data sources and types is another big challenge in the implementation of big data analytics. It is a big challenge to standardize datasets, policies, languages and clinical standards. Interoperability also requires developing common interfaces, recording health information and defining quality healthcare standards.

References

Bhatt, V., & Chakraborty, S. (2021). Real-time healthcare monitoring using smart systems: A step towards healthcare service orchestration. In *Proceedings of the international conference on artificial intelligence and smart systems (ICAIS-2021)* (pp. 772–777). IEEE.

Bi, H., Liu, J., & Kato, N.(2022). Deep learning-based privacy preservation and data analytics for IoT enabled healthcare. *IEEE Transactions on Industrial Informatics, 18*(7), 4798–4807.

Chakraborty, S., Aich, S., & Kim, H. C.(2019). A Secure Healthcare System Design Framework using Blockchain Technology. *International Conference on Advanced Communications Technology(ICACT)* (pp. 260–264).

Galletta, A., Carnevale, L., Bramanti, A., & Fazio, M.(2019). An innovative methodology for big data visualization for telemedicine. *IEEE Transactions on Industrial Informatics, 15*(1), 490–497.

Ghayvat, H., Pandya, S., Bhattacharya, P., Zuhair, M., Rashid, M., Hakak, S., & Dev, K.(2022). CP-BDHCA: Blockchain-based confidentiality-privacy preserving big data scheme for healthcare clouds and applications. *IEEE Journal of Biomedical and Health Informatics, 26*(5), 1937–1948.

Hirata, S. (2020). Designing sustainable healthcare service based on dynamic extraction of requirements hidden from User's language. *2nd IEEE Eurasia Conference on Biomedical Engineering, Healthcare and Sustainability* (pp. 145–146). IEEE.

Hooda, M., Ramesh, M., Gupta, A., Nair, J., & Nandanan, K.(2021). Need assessment and design of an IoT based healthcare solution through participatory approaches for a rural village in Bihar, India. *IEEE 9th Region 10 Humanitarian Technology Conference (R10-HTC)* (pp. 1–6). IEEE.

Husain, M. S. (2019). Social Media Analytics to predict depression level in the users. In Sudip Paul, Pallab Bhattacharya, Arindam Bit (Eds.) *Early detection of neurological disorders using machine learning systems* (pp. 199–215). IGI Global.

Husain, M. S., Adnan, M. H. B. M., Khan, M. Z., Shukla, S., & Khan, F. U.(2022). *Pervasive healthcare.* Springer International Publishing.

Imran, S., Mahmood, T., Morshed, A., & Sellis, T.(2021). Big data analytics in healthcare — A systematic literature review and roadmap for practical implementation. *IEEE/CAA Journal of Automatica Sinica, 8*(1), 1–22.

Jayanthilladevi, A., Sangeetha, K., & Balamurugan, E. (2020). Healthcare biometrics security and regulations: Biometrics data security and regulations governing PHI and HIPAA act for patient privacy. *2020 International Conference on Emerging Smart Computing and Informatics (ESCI)* (pp. 244–247).

Jindal, A., Dua, A., Kumar, N., Das, A. K., Vasilakos, A. V., & Rodrigues, J. J. (2018). Providing healthcare-as-a-service using fuzzy rule based big data analytics in cloud computing. *IEEE Journal of Biomedical and Health Informatics, 22*(5), 1605–1618.

Khan, A., Husain, M. S., Khan, A.(2018). Analysis of mental state of users using social media to predict depression! A survey. *International Journal of Advanced Research in Computer Science, 9*(2), 100–106.

Lambay, M. A., & Mohideen, S. P.(2020). Big data analytics for healthcare recommendation systems. *International Conference on System, Computation, Automation and Networking (ICSCAN)* (pp. 1–6). IEEE.

Li, C., & Xu, S.(2020). Interaction design for smart healthcare system considering older adults' healthy and wellbeing lifestyles. *2nd IEEE Eurasia Conference on Biomedical Engineering, Healthcare and Sustainability* (pp. 151–153). IEEE.

Naveed, N., Madhloom, H. T., & Husain, M. S. (2021). Breast cancer diagnosis using wrapper-based feature selection and artificial neural network. *Applied Computer Science, 17*(3), 19–30.

Nazir, S., Nawaz, M., Adnan, A., Shahzad, S., & Asadi, S.(2019). Big data features, applications, and analytics in cardiology—A systematic literature review. *IEEE Access, 7,* 143742–143771.

Philip, N. Y., Razaak, M., Chang, J., O'Kane, M., & Pierscionek, B. K. (2022). A data analytics suite for exploratory predictive, and visual analysis of Type 2 diabetes. *IEEE Access,* 13460–13471.

Raja, R., Mukherjee, I., & Sarkar, B. K.(2020). A systematic review of healthcare big data. *Scientific Programming, 2020,* 1–15.

Tariq, S., Akhtar, N., Afzal, H., Khalid, S., Mufti, M. R., Hussain, S., Habib, A., & Ahmad, G.(2019). A novel co-training-based approach for he classification of mental illnesses using social media posts. *IEEE Access,* 166165–166172.

Yu, Y., Li, M., Liu, L., Li, Y., & Wang, J.(2019). Clinical big data and deep learning: Applications, challenges, and future outlooks. *Big Data Mining and Analytics, 2*(4),288–305.

Tripathi, M. M., Haroon, M., Khan, Z., & Husain, M. S. (2022). Security in Digital Healthcare System. In M. S. Husain, M. H. B. M. Adnan, M. Z. Khan, S. Shukla, & F. U. Khan (Eds.), *Pervasive Healthcare* (pp. 217–231). Springer.

Zhou, S., He, J., Yang, H., Chen, D., & Zhang, R.(2020). Big data-driven abnormal behavior detection in healthcare based on association rules. *IEEE Access, 8,* 129002–129011.

Chapter 10

Big Data Analytics for Fraud Detection

10.1 Introduction

With the advent of sophisticated techniques and developments in electronic devices most industries, including telecommunication, government agencies, healthcare, insurance, banking, e-commerce, etc., are adopting digitization to improve productivity and better facilitate their users. These online systems can be used by anyone (including both legitimate users as well as fraudsters); hence they are becoming more vulnerable to large-scale and systematic fraud.

The term fraud means to acquire money, goods or services in unethical or illegal ways. Almost all technological systems that involve money, services and personal information can be compromised by fraudulent acts. Fraudulent activities are of critical concern because of their severe impact on organizations and communities as well as individuals, causing huge amounts of financial losses. Because of its criticality, this problem has encouraged researchers to develop models to detect fraud and prevent fraud or estimate fraud risk (Siddiqui et al., 2018).

DOI: 10.1201/9781003441595-13

Traditionally machine learning and statistics have been implemented for fraud detection and prevention, but unfortunately these approaches have several limitations. Significantly, big data analytics can help industries in discovering hidden patterns and make an important contribution during process examination and facilitate the detection of irregularities (Verma et al., 2018).

10.2 Types of Fraud

There are different types of fraudulent activities depending on the industry sector. Fraudsters not only attack banks but also other industries like insurance, government agencies, healthcare and telecommunications (Tarannum & Husain, 2017). According to the Global Economic Crime and Fraud Survey (PwC, 2022), in the past two years 46% of the surveyed organizations have experienced one or another kind of fraud. These fraudulent acts cause millions of dollars in damages as well as brand damage, loss of market position, damage to employee morale and loss of future opportunities. Examples of fraud include, but are not limited to the following (Abdallahn et al., 2016).

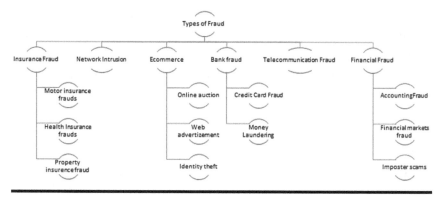

Figure 10.1   Types of fraud.

10.2.1 Insurance Fraud

Insurance systems are intended to support individuals and to cover losses and to protect against risks. Fraud occurs when the insured individual uses the insurance contract as a tool to gain illegal profit. An insurance system involves different parties such as policyholders, agents and brokers, insurance companies and banks. In addition, the system implements many rules and regulations. The involvement of so many different parties makes it easy for fraudsters to do illegal and unethical acts, and also the complicated system and regulations make it harder to discover fraudulent activities. Different types of insurance fraud are motor insurance fraud, health insurance fraud and property insurance fraud.

10.2.2 Network Intrusion

Hackers or fraudsters gain unauthorized access to a network or machine and may harm the system or steal key information to commit fraud (Husain, 2020; Akbar et al., 2020).

10.2.3 Credit Card Fraud

The two common types of credit card fraud are application fraud and transaction fraud. Other types of credit card fraud include bankruptcy fraud, counterfeit fraud, theft fraud and behavioral fraud. Fraudsters can apply and get a credit card by using fake or stolen identity details. Most of the time, fraudsters gain unauthorized access to individuals' credit card information and make online purchases or money transactions.

10.2.4 Money Laundering

In money laundering, law offenders or crooked people try to transact money while disguising the source of money because it is not from legitimate sources and is gained through illegal activities. The impact of money laundering is very dangerous because it is the main pillar of various criminal activities like terrorism financing, arms trading and child, organ and drug trafficking. Tracking money laundering is a very complex challenge because it is governed by multiple social and economic conditions.

10.2.5 Accounting Fraud

An official report that reflects the financial activities and position of a business is called a financial statement. Accounting fraud can be viewed as a deliberate misquotation of financial statements with the intention of misleading investors and creditors, and to create a false impression of an organization's strength.

10.2.6 Financial Markets Fraud

The securities market in any economy is the place where prices of financial instruments like stocks and bonds, etc., are determined on the basis of demand and supply and parties can buy and sell them. Financial markets fraud, also known as securities fraud or investment fraud, refers to misleading practices by individuals or organizations that induce financiers to make purchase or sale decisions on the basis of false information.

10.2.7 Telecommunication Fraud

In telecommunications, fraud is characterized by the abusive use of any carrier services without the intention of paying, for example sim cloning. Telecommunication fraud can be committed with fixed and mobile telephone lines, and this problem has grown dramatically in recent years. Different types of telecommunication fraud are contractual fraud, hacking fraud and technical fraud.

10.3 Fraud Detection and Prevention

Detecting, preventing and eliminating fraud are the key concerns of industries at present. The main approaches for fraud detection and prevention can be categorized as shown in Figure 10.2.

10.3.1 Traditional Fraud Detection Methods

The traditional methods are only effective in simple cases with little data analysis and consume a lot of time and human effort. With the exponential growth in digital data, the analysis capacity of traditional methods is not enough.

10.3.1.1 Discrete Analysis

These methods depend on discrete analysis performed on structured data. Rule-based algorithms are used to detect suspicious actions which are then manually reviewed by investigators. The major drawbacks of such an approach are the time it takes, human errors and the inability to identify irregular and unusual patterns of behavior that could result in fraud.

10.3.1.2 Ad-Hoc Analysis and Sampling

Ad-hoc analysis aims to detect specific information about a particular event by testing random transactions for possible malicious activity. Ad-hoc testing is based on formulas and queries that require manual labor and is time-consuming. Sampling techniques often complement ad-hoc analysis by providing samples of transactions with fraud risks that can point out some eccentricities. These methods show good results on small datasets but aren't that effective on overwhelming data volumes (Nikolaienko, 2022).

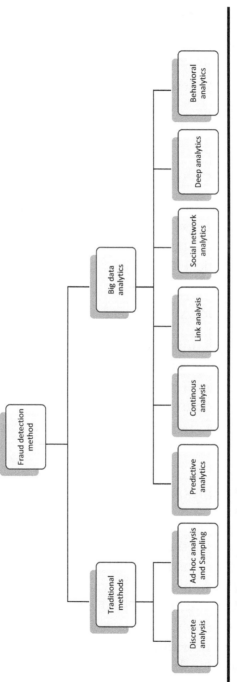

Figure 10.2 Fraud detection methods.

10.3.2 Big Data Analytics for Fraud Detection

Big data analytics is quite effective in detecting fraud by analyzing consumers' current patterns, behavior history and transaction methods and identifying anomalies. Big data analytics is fairly cost-effective, fast, accurate and efficient in fraud detection and risk identification.

103.2.1 Predictive Analytics

Predictive analytics aims to implement a machine learning model that is used to predict the incidence of any suspicious or fraudulent activity and the risk involved. Predictive analysis makes use of historical data to train the model.

10.3.2.2 Continuous Analysis

Most fraud cases go unnoticed for a long time. Continuous analysis allows its users to consistently monitor transactions and user activities for a longer period of time (in months). The major strength of continuous analytics is the opportunity to provide new insights based on its findings compared to the more conventional rule-based approach.

10.3.2.3 Link Analysis

With the increase and diversification of data, a lot of valuable information related to customer behavior is hidden in the streams of real-time unstructured data including text, voice, pictures, mouse movements and gyro sensor readings. Link analysis is based on network visualization where the data items are represented as a connected graph. Link analysis is very effective in providing a bigger picture of connected behaviors and relationships between different entities like individuals, IP addresses, payment methods or browsing history that helps in identifying potential fraudulent activities.

10.3.2.4 Social Network Analytics (SNA)

Social network analysis is a kind of link analysis which provides useful insights into larger datasets of social networks based on the correlation of the analyzed entities. Social network analysis expands the scope of valuable data by extracting additional value in real time from linking various data sources for predictive analysis.

10.3.2.5 Deep Analytics

Deep analytics techniques detect anomalies and flag potentially fraudulent activity by analyzing the behavioral patterns of users. Deep analytics systems spot the trends and relationships between similar attacks and create real-time algorithms for identifying fraudulent activities.

10.3.2.6 Behavioral Analytics

These algorithms build user profiles by collecting relevant information like type of device, location, mode of transaction, pattern of interaction, mouse movements and clicks over a period of time. When an interaction occurs, the current information is evaluated against the user's profile. Behavioral analytics are quite efficient in examining the exact nature of the interaction between users and banking websites, and distinguishing between fraud and genuine unusual activities.

10.4 Features Used for Fraud Detection

There are various parameters like user IP address, email, frequency of transactions, etc. These features can be categorized as follows.

Table 10.1 Features for Fraud Detection

Feature	Example
Traditional features	Transaction details, mode of payment, location, etc.
Real-time features	IP address, card details, country, etc.
Individual behavioral features	Browsing history, frequency of transactions, time spent on a particular page, etc.
Entity features	Device used, IP address, domains, emails, etc.
Link analysis features	Entities in the network, relationship between these entities

10.5 Benefits of Big Data Analytics for Fraud Detection

The key benefit of using data analytics for fraud detection is that these systems can process huge volumes of data with ease. By analyzing large amounts of relevant data, these systems can identify the trends and possible glitches substantially faster than traditional methods. Some of the benefits of using big data analytics for fraud detection include:

- Easily acquire, normalize, merge and compare data from different systems
- Automatically identify the indicators for fraud detection
- Automate the complete process of monitoring and detection
- Reduce the risk of sampling errors and improves internal controls
- Speed up fraud analysis by eliminating manual work
- Identify fraud before it occurs
- Accurately calculate the impact of fraud

- Ensure a high fraud detection rate removing false positives
- Save costs and maximize revenue
- Help identify and fix weaknesses in the system

10.6 Applications of Big Data Analytics for Fraud Detection

Almost every public or private industry is susceptible to one or another kind of fraud, but data analytics helps in the detection of the fraud and in providing a mitigating solution for the fraud. Some of the key areas where data analytics is effective in fraud detection are:

- Dealing with bank frauds like fake or compromised accounts
- Detecting fraud in the pharmaceutical industry
- Spotting identity fraud/imposter scam
- Preventing credit card fraud
- Identifying insurance fraud
- Taking down organized crime
- Fraud detection in taxation
- Detecting money laundering
- Managing fraudulent behavior in e-commerce
- Financial fraud detection
- Email scams
- Data breaches

10.7 Issues in Implementing Big Data Analytics for Fraud Detection

Although big data analytics has shown promising results in fraud detection, still many organizations hesitate to incorporate big data analytics methods in their process because of various challenges. Some of the key issues which these organizations may face are:

- Insufficient data for training purposes: The efficiency of any machine learning-based system depends on the quality and quantity of the training data. More training data implies better performance. Acquiring significant amounts of data for training fraud detection systems is hard because of challenges like privacy, security and lack of rules.
- Integrating a variety of data from multiple heterogeneous sources: For big data analytics, the data is acquired from multiple heterogeneous sources. To preprocess this huge volume of data and make it application ready is a complex task.
- Dynamic patterns of fraud: Hackers and criminals vary their strategies of attack by spotting vulnerable points in the system. The defense system needs to be regularly updated using sophisticated techniques to counter these dynamic attacks.
- Lack of skilled professionals: Industries lack professionals who are skilled and experienced enough to implement the appropriate model effectively for application-specific fraud detection and prevention.
- Ineffectiveness of traditional rule-based methods: The traditional models built on rule-based models were not very effective and consumed a lot of human effort. This performance has discouraged industries from adopting big data analytics in their system.
- High costs: Acquiring the huge amount of data needed and handling it as part of the analytical process requires sophisticated tools, techniques and trained professionals which incur high costs.
- Real-time fraud detection: Analyzing the transaction patterns in real-time data streaming to spot anomalies

and flag possible suspicious activities is a very complex task.

- ▪ Skewed class distribution: There are various classes of fraud depending on the targeted industry. Unbalanced classes of frauds make it difficult to build an effective machine learning model.
- ▪ Performance measure: Although machine learning models are very effective in anomaly detection, meaning identifying abnormal behavior or unexpected activities, the actual performance of these system depends on the data and technique used. For optimal performance we need relevant quality data to build the model by selecting the most appropriate learning approach.
- ▪ Unsuccessful experience: Because of unplanned, improper implementation, many industries have failed in implementing fraud detection systems in the past and now they are doubtful of the success of big data analytics.

References

Abdallah, A., Maarof, M. A., & Zainal, A.(2016). Fraud detection system: A survey. *Journal of Network and Computer Applications, 68*, 90–113.

Akbar, M., Suaib, M., Husain, M. S., & Shukla, S.(2020). A compendium of cloud forensics. In Mohammad Shahid Husain, Mohammad Zunnun Khan (Eds.) *Critical concepts, standards, and techniques in cyber forensics* (pp. 215–227). IGI Global.

Husain, M. S. (2020). Nature inspired approach for intrusion detection systems. In Dinesh Goyal, S. Balamurugan, Sheng-Lung Peng, O. P. Verma (Eds.) *Design and analysis of security protocol for communication* (pp. 171–182). John Wiley & Sons.

Nikolaienko, O. (2022). *Financial fraud detection powered by big data analytics*. Retrieved from https://www.infopulse.com: https://www.infopulse.com/blog/financial-fraud-detection -powered-by-big-data#:~:text=When%20only%20Google%20pro- cesses%2020,help%20spot%20potential%20fraudulent%20 activities

PwC. (2022). *Global economic crime and fraud survey.* PwC Network.

Siddiqui, M. Z., Yadav, S., & Husain, M. S.(2018). Application of artificial intelligence in fighting against cyber crimes: A review. *International Journal of Advanced Research in Computer Science, 9*(2), 118–122.

Tarannum, S., & Husain, S.(2017). Opinion mining with spam detection using real time data on cloud. *International Journal of Advanced Research in Computer Science, 8*(7), 910–914.

Verma, A., Arif, M., & Husain, M. S. (2018). Analysis of DDOS attack detection and prevention in cloud environment: A review. *International Journal of Advanced Research in Computer Science, 9*, 107–113.

Chapter 11

Big Data Analytics in Social Media

11.1 Introduction

Social media are Internet-based interaction platforms that enable users to post content that can be instantaneously edited and amended and allow people to share information with each another. Social media platforms are increasing in popularity as users feel free to share their thoughts on different topics (including controversial ones) with intended groups or the general public in a faster and easier manner. With millions of users across the globe and the gigantic amount of real-time content generation social media serve as an effective instrument in raising public awareness, especially during pandemics and emergency situations. The exponential amount of data generated by different social media platforms as shown in Figure 11.1 has opened up a valuable data source for both academia and industry to extract meaningful insights, for example what people think about a certain policy, a product, a person, a place or an idea.

DOI: 10.1201/9781003441595-14

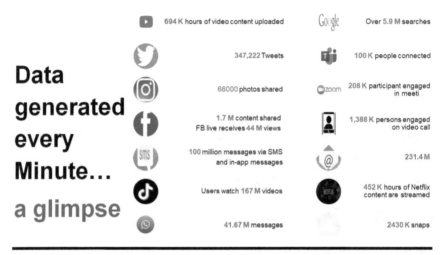

Figure 11.1 Data generation through social media platforms (Data Never Sleeps 10.0, 2022).

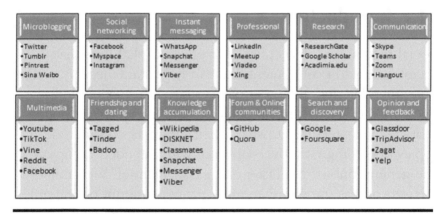

Figure 11.2 Types of social media platforms.

11.2 Types of Social Media Platforms

Social media platforms are used for various purposes like building professional connections, sharing opinions about certain topics, making friends and interacting with them, technical discussions and knowledge sharing, communicating with friends or business partners and contributing knowledge. Based on the type of content generated, social media can be categorized into different types as shown in Figure 11.2.

11.3 Social Media Statistics

Exponential growth in the use of social media has transformed our ordinary lives. Individuals and organizations use social media for making new contacts, building professional relationships, following a brand, getting information about different products or services, sharing opinions, etc. In January 2023 there were 4.76 billion users on social media which is around 59.5% of the total population of the world. Facebook generates around four petabytes of data every day (Vuleta, 2021). Approximately 2.5 quintillion bytes of data is generated every day (Prodanoff, 2022), and this is expected to reach 463 exabytes per day by 2025 (Bulao, 2022).

Some of the key statistics regarding social media usage are shown in Figures 11.3 and 11.4.

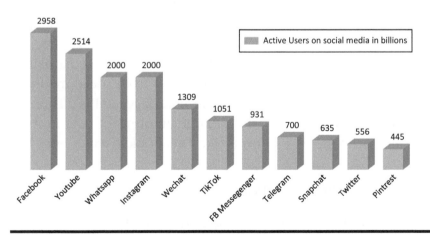

Figure 11.3   Active users (in billions) on social media (Global Social Media Statistics, 2023).

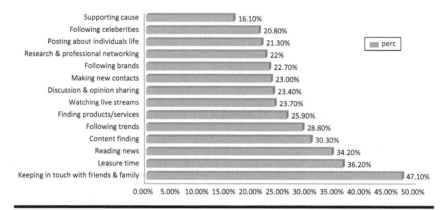

Figure 11.4   Reason for social media usage (Global Social Media Statistics, 2023).

11.4 Big Data Analytics in Social Media

The huge volume of data available through social media can help businesses in making well-informed decisions and strategy planning. This has ignited a lot of interest in industries in making use of big data analytics on social media and in getting meaningful insights from the content shared every day by billions of users in the form of text, image, audio, video, gif, blog, etc. However, it is necessary to incorporate effective and appropriate analytical procedures and tools to analyze the ever-increasing data acquired from various social media platforms. One can acquire this valuable data from social media platforms using application program interfaces (APIs). These APIs allow easy public access to large amounts of data from specific social media platforms like Facebook, Twitter, etc.

11.4.1 Analytic Techniques

Researchers have explored various data analytics approaches to extract insights from the huge volumes of data gathered from social media platforms to facilitate different business purposes. A novel framework for analyzing tweets to extract the topic of the tweets and their sentiment towards a particular topic (specifically controversial) has been proposed by Pouria Babvey et al. (2021). An embedded approach of utilizing geospatial emotion vectors with graph theory, machine learning and statistics has been developed by Brandon Lwowski et al. (2020) for tracking trending topics during times of extreme emotion. The research team of Sahraoui Dhelim et al. (2021) has implemented social-oriented machinelearning and deeplearning techniques to explore the impact of IoT in social relationship management. An effective approach to relieving social problems using positive as well as negative influences was presented by Jing (Selena) He et al. (2019). Social media analytics-oriented problems and their solutions using deep learning has been discussed by Malik Khizar Hayat et al. (2019). A dynamic clustering algorithm for the real-time visual analysis of high-volume social media posts has been proposed by Johannes Knittel et al. (2022). Blockchain-enabled explainable federated learning for securing Internet-of-things-based social media 3.0 networks has been proposed by Sara Salim et al. (2021). A hybrid fuzzy multi-objective optimization algorithm is used by Arun Kumar Sangaiah et al. (2020) for the optimization of social media analytics. In general, the social media analytics techniques can be categorized based on the type of content, the purpose of analysis and the approach used (Hou et al., 2020) as shown in Figure 11.5. Text mining, graph theory, opinion mining, search engine optimization, social influence analysis, opinion mining, cyber risk analysis and others are some of the diverse approaches to big data analytics in social media. Figure 11.6 represents a snapshot of how much these analytic techniques are used.

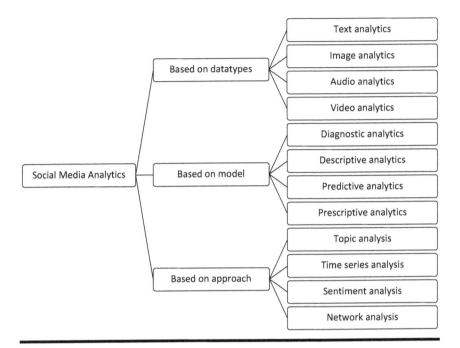

Figure 11.5   Social media analytic approaches.

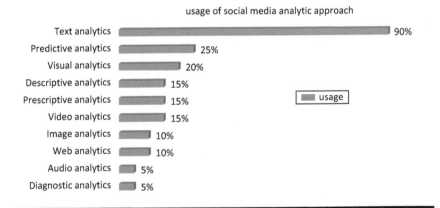

Figure 11.6   Usage of social media analytic approaches (Md. Saifur Rahman, 2022).

11.4.1.1 Social Media Analytics Based on Data Type

- **Text analytics**: In text analytics, natural language application-based techniques are used to analyze textual data on social media like reviews, comments, posts, etc.
- **Image analytics**: A lot of social media users post different pictures, photographs or images related to some event, product or trip. Researchers analyze these pictorial contents to get valuable insights.
- **Audio analytics**: Voice messages, audio recordings, speeches or music are analyzed using machine learning to extract meaningful information from social media.
- **Video analytics**: Video analytics is the latest trend where video content uploaded by social media users is analyzed to extract valuable information.

11.4.1.2 Social Media Analytics Based on Model

- **Descriptive analytics**: Descriptive analytics is done to analyze social media content to monitor events and identify the current trends to better understand the business scenario.
- **Diagnostic analytics**: Diagnostic analytics helps in identifying the cause behind a particular trend by using data correlation and the coherency between social media content.
- **Predictive analytics**: Predictive data analytic models help in forecasting future possibilities by analyzing historical social media content and identifying particular patterns or trends.
- **Prescriptive analytics**: Prescriptive data analytics is used to identify the optimal course of action in a particular scenario by analyzing the archived content and evaluating all of the future possibilities.

11.4.1.3 Social Media Analytics Based on Approach

■ **Topic analysis**: To identify the current trends or hot topics of discussion among the users on social media, researchers make use of hashtags, queries or specific models (topic models). These abstract topics are very helpful in getting meaningful insight relevant to business.

■ **Time series analysis**: Social media uploads contain information about various types of events. Time series analytics is based on analyzing data with timestamps. This helps in identifying different aspects of the event like peaks and drops in sales, the correlation between different events, irregular or unpredictable scenarios, seasonal variations and future trends.

■ **Sentiment analysis**: Sentiment analysis or opinion mining aims to identify the opinion or sentiment polarity of users related to a particular topic, policy or product. Sentiment analysis helps in improved decision making regarding a product or policy.

■ **Network analysis**: In network analysis, the users and the relation between them are visualized as nodes and edges in a social network. Analyzing social networks gives a lot of information, for example on social media influencers and how different entities in the network are related to each other.

11.5 Applications of Big Data Analytics in Social Media

Social media content is proving to be one of the premium sources of big data which is easily available for analysis. The various impacts of social media analytics are represented in Figure 11.7.

Almost all sectors including government, manufacturing industries, research, finance, defense, healthcare, politics, banking,

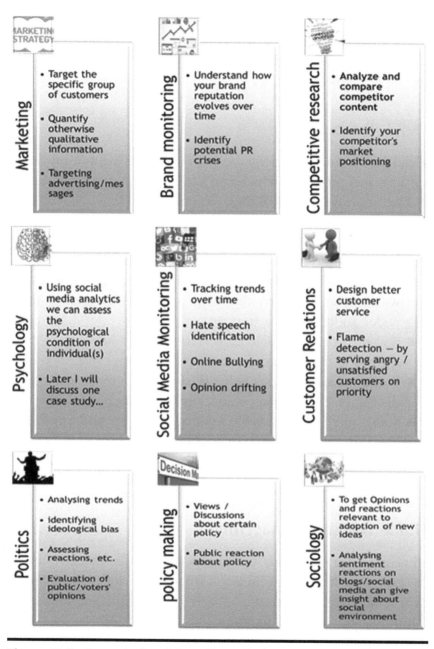

Figure 11.7 Impact of social media analytics.

telecommunications, sociology, public transport systems, marketing and insurance make use of social media analytics to get insight into current trends and prepare for the future. Some of the key applications of social media analytics are as follows.

11.5.1 Business

Social media analytics helps businesses get user input on their services and products, which can be used to make changes and get more value out of their brand.

- Social media platforms enable consumers to share their feedback and register complaints directly.
- Viral marketing is becoming cheaper, more efficient and widespread. Social media helps publicize information to a wider audience in a short time.
- Social media analytics helps businesses to better plan their new products or services.
- Social media analytics helps businesses to make strategic decisions for targeted promotions of their products.
- Social media analytics for making strategies and improving customer relationships is used by almost all of the business giants like Microsoft, Facebook, Amazon, Apple and Samsung.

11.5.2 Disaster Management

Witnessing the enormous usage of social media, researchers are exploring it as a real-time information broadcasting platform which can be treated as a new avenue of decentralized communication during disasters.

- Social media can be effective in providing a real-time disaster response.
- Social media analytics can help in providing awareness about the latest situation in disaster-affected areas.

- Social media analytics can help in disseminating information about missing people and contacting family members.
- Governing bodies can make corrective decisions in time and also widely publicize them for public awareness.

11.5.3 Healthcare

Social media-based bio-surveillance systems can be used as early warning systems for upcoming public health emergencies. Social media analytics is also useful in identifying mental stress and depression levels in users (Husain, 2019).

- Social media analytics with IoT can contribute to effective pervasive healthcare.
- Social media analytics is helpful in tracking progress towards specific goals like vaccination for COVID-19.
- Social media analytics can help in monitoring the frequency and pattern of a particular disease.
- Social media analytics can be used to identify causes and possible risks of health-related issues in specified localities.
- Social media analytics helps governing bodies in evidence-based decision making by identifying risk factors for disease and targeting preventive healthcare.
- Social media analytics helps governing bodies in setting priorities and disseminating information regarding public health policies and strategies.

11.5.4 Governance

Federal or state governments use social data analytics effectively to develop predictive decisions.

- Social media analytics can help governments in identifying unemployment status and making relevant policies.
- Social media analytics helps governments to find out public sentiments about certain policies or decisions.

- Social media analytics helps in identifying antisocial elements and countering terrorism.
- Social media analytics helps in effective policy making and improving e-governance.
- Social media analytics is also helpful in congestion and traffic control.
- Political parties frequently use sentiment and opinion mining during sensitive events like local or national election processes.
- Social media analytics can help in understanding evolving situations and providing a quick response.

11.6 Key Challenges in Social Media Analytics

Some of the key challenges in effectively implementing social media analytics are:

- **Data privacy**: Although most social media platforms are public, accessing individuals' profiles and posts is not easy because of privacy constraints.
- **Multimedia content**: A lot of social media content is comprised of multimedia like audio, videos and images which require sophisticated techniques and complex tasks for processing and analysis.
- **Noisy data**: The data volume from social media is exponentially increasing with an unimaginable number of posts per second. However, most of this data is not useful for targeted applications, and a lot of effort is required in filtering and cleaning the data to make it application ready.
- **Data integration**: For useful insights, instead of using only one platform, there is a need to acquire input data from multiple sources. Integrating data from multiple heterogeneous sources is a complex task.
- **Rumor and fake news**: Especially in recent times, a lot of rumors and fake news circulate on social media

platforms. Using data without verifying its authenticity and genuineness leads to the wrong results and affects decision making.

■ **Multilingual support**: Social media platforms are global and the content is multilingual. To make the most of social media analytics, the models used should support multiple languages.

■ **Cyberattacks**: Social media platforms are quite vulnerable to cyberattacks, especially during sensitive events.

References

Babvey, P., Borrelli, D., Lipizzi, C., & Ramirez-Marquez, J. E. (2021). Content-aware galaxies: Digital fingerprints of discussions on social media. *IEEE Transactions on Computational Social Systems, 8*(2),294–307.

Bulao, J. (2022). *How much data is created every day in 2022?* techjury.net. Retrieved from https://techjury.net/blog/how-much -data-is-created-every-day/

Dhelim, S., Ning, H., Farha, F., Chen, L., Atzori, L., & Daneshmand, M.. (2021). IoT-enabled social relationships meet artificial social intelligence. *IEEE Internet of Things Journal, 8*(24), 17817–17828.

Hayat, M. K., Daud, A., Alshdadi, A. A., Banjar, A., Abbasi, R. A., Bao, Y., & Dawood, H. (2019). Towards deep learning prospects: Insights for social Media Analytics. *IEEE Access, 7,*36958–36979.

He, J. S., Han, M., Ji, S., Du, T., & Li, Z. (2019). Spreading social influence with both positive and negative opinions in online networks. *Big Data Mining and Analytics, 2*(2),100–117.

Hou, Q., Han, M., & Cai, Z.. (2020). Survey on data analysis in social media: A practical application aspect. *Big Data Mining and Analytics, 3*(4), 259–279.

Husain, M. S. (2019). Social Media Analytics to predict depression level in the users. In Sudip Paul, Pallab Bhattacharya, Arindam Bit (Eds.)*Early detection of neurological disorders using machine learning systems* (pp. 199–215). IGI Global.

Knittel, J., Koch, S., Tang, T., Chen, W., Wu, Y., Liu, S., & Ertl, T. (2022). Real-time visual analysis of high-volume social media posts. *IEEE Transactions on Visualization and Computer Graphics, 28*(1), 879–889.

Lwowski, B., Rad, P., & Choo, K. K. R. (2020). Geospatial event detection by grouping emotion contagion in social media. *IEEE Transactions on Big Data, 6*(1),159–170.

Prodanoff, J. T. (2022). *How much data is created every day in 2022.* webtribunal.net. Retrieved from https://webtribunal.net/blog/how-much-data-is-created-every-day/

Rahman, M. S., & Reza, H. (2022). A systematic review towards big data analytics in social media. *Big Data Mining and Analytics, 5*(3), 228–244.

Salim, S., Turnbull, B., & Moustafa, N. (2021). A blockchain-enabled explainable federated learning for securing Internet-of-things-based social Media 3.0 networks. *IEEE Transactions on Computational Social Systems.*

Sangaiah, A. K., Goli, A., Tirkolaee, E. B., Ranjbar-Bourani, M., Pandey, H. M., & Zhang, W. (2020). Big data-driven cognitive computing system for optimization of social Media Analytics. *IEEE Access, 8*, 82215–82226.

Vuleta, B. (2021). *How much data is created every day? +27 staggering stats.* Retrieved from https://seedscientific.com/: https://seedscientific.com/how-much-data-is-created-every-day/

Data Never Sleeps 10.0. (2022). Retrieved from https://www.domo.com/learn/data-never-sleeps-10. Domo.

(2023). *Global social media statistics.* Kepios: Datareportal.

Chapter 12

Novel Applications and Research Directions in Big Data Analytics

12.1 Introduction

Recent advances in technologies like cloud computing, sensor networks, social media platforms, smart phones, the Internet of Things (IoT), the medical Internet of Things (MIoT), the industry Internet of Things (IIoT), body sensor networks (BSN), etc., have impacted almost all the industries and sectors whether public or private. Big data analytics is the latest trend, and every industry is adopting it to improve performance and strategy making and to remain competitive.

12.2 Education Sector

The success of big data analytics in traditional business applications has encouraged researchers to explore and incorporate big data analytics in the education industry (Liu, 2020). A Multi-Attention Fusion Model (Multi-AFM) was proposed

DOI: 10.1201/9781003441595-15

by Guanlin Zhai (2020) to analyze the sentiments of students regarding the heavy workload of the curriculum. Munshi (2021) has proposed a comprehensive Big Data Platform for Educational Analytics. Different aspects of big data analytics in education, like educational platforms, big data analytic architectures and data analytics approaches for big education data, are summarized by Kenneth Li-Minn Ang et al. in their survey work (Ang, 2020). Big data analytics can provide effective support in the education industry in various ways, for example:

- **Enrollment/retention**: Targeting prospective students for admission and identifying underprepared students when they enter campus.
- **Collaborative learning**: Students preference analysis, social network analysis and discovering patterns of academic collaboration.
- **Pedagogical support**: Easy to adapt new trends, course design based on future market needs, helping students identify majors related to their interests and mapping courses to achieve their degree and providing support for self-learning.
- **Student monitoring**: Identifying learning gaps, efficiency, deficiency, participation and behavioral analysis.
- **Welfare support**: Identifying students who need moral support and students who need financial support.

12.3 Agriculture Sector

With the use of advanced technologies like cloud computing, IoT and sensor networks, big data analytics plays a major role in providing food security and improving the agriculture sector (Araújo, 2021). In the era of climate change, increasing urbanization, land and water constraints and changing income and diet patterns it is highly important to ensure nutrition security for the ever increasing population. Soil and land resources can be used optimally by making use of big data and the Internet of Things, combined with remote sensing (RS) and geographic information systems (GIS) (Chen, 2020). Big data analytics also helps in analyzing the environmental factors of farming and enabling better crop selection (Tseng, 2019) and the development of expert systems to assist farmers in crop selection and planning their production (Singh, 2018). The impact and challenges of AI techniques with IoT in agriculture was discussed by Singh et al. (2021) and Bhat (2021) in their survey articles. The advent of cloud computing has enabled the availability of high computing power and easy access to huge data sources which can be effectively used to provide important knowledge such as weather, irrigation practices, plant nutrient requirements and several other farming techniques to everyone whenever needed. The key impacts of big data analytics on agriculture are:

- Crop estimation
- Improved yields and profitability
- Precision farming
- Administration of pesticides
- Development of new seed traits
- Production based on market demand
- Optimizing farm equipment
- Spoilage and food-borne illnesses prevention
- Managing supply chain issues
- Sustainable utilization of soil and land resources

12.4 Entertainment Industry

The recent work on big data analytics in entertainment industries includes understanding music-related brain activity (Ntalampiras, 2019), an attempt to propose a framework for personalized music generation (Hu, 2022), a novel approach to music emotion recognition in live music performance (Yang,

2021), automatic music genre classification (Pelchat, 2020), personalized recommendations of film and television resources (Miao, 2022; Wang, 2020), analyzing users' comments to get more insights about a particular movie (Li, 2018), a novel framework for starring character identification in movies (Haq, 2019) and many other prominent works. In general, big data analytics in entertainment is helpful in the following ways:

- Customer satisfaction and retention
- Personalized recommendations
- Identifying starring characters in movies
- Analyzing performance based on the users' reviews and comments
- Movie/music genre classification
- Analyzing the role of gender, personality and audio features in movies or music
- Predicting weekend box office
- Identifying emotions in movie scripts
- Movie poster genre classification

12.5 Manufacturing

Important applications of big data analytics in manufacturing industries include:

- **Product quality control**: Big data analytics can be very effective in the automation of product quality control processes.
- **Revenue performance**: By incorporating big data analytics in the process and decision making, industry can positively improve its revenue.
- **Maintenance forecasting**: With big data analytics using historical data and circumstantial factors, industries can better forecast the health of machinery and can predict when and which tools/machines need maintenance.

12.6 Renewable Energy

Important applications of big data analytics in the renewable energy sector include:

- **Energy forecasting**: Using historical data and current requirements, big data analytics can help in predicting future energy requirements like electricity requirements in a particular region during the next year, and the agencies can better prepare themselves.
- **Predictive maintenance**: Big data analytics can predict possible issues that may happen in the future like grid failure and help in taking measures in time.
- **Pricing**: Big data analytics can help in appropriate pricing by analyzing the demand and supply in the future.

12.7 Business Applications

Important applications of big data analytics in business industries include:

- **Customer profiling:** Using big data analytics, business can categorize their customers based on various parameters which help in providing customized services.
- **Supply chain management**: Big data analytics can be helpful in managing the supply chain end to end from the service provider to the end users.
- **Targeted marketing**: Big data analytics is used to identify the preferences of individuals and catagorize the customers profiles by businesses to target them for marketing their product.
- **Logistics**: Logistics is one of the key components for the success of any business. In recent years researchers have focused on improving the logistic process and big data analytics can be very helpful in this task.

- **E-commerce**: Big data analytics can contribute to improving and managing various aspects of e-commerce like product recommendations, countering unethical or illegal activities and understanding the customer's sentiments.
- **CRM**: Customer relationship management aims to provide the best services to customers, resolve their complaints, implement policies to retain customers for longer and attract new customers. Big data analytics can help businesses in achieving the above tasks in an efficient manner and satisfy their customers.

12.8 Financial Services

Important applications of big data analytics in financial sectors include:

- **Stock exchange prediction**: By analyzing the historical patterns of stocks, big data analytics helps in accurately predicting the future trends of commodity stocks.
- **Credit score-based loan/credit card approval**: Based on the customer's profile and other historical data, big data analytics can easily categorize a person as a defaulter or not. This helps financial institutions and banks to approve/disapprove any loan or credit card application or to decide the loan/credit amount limit.
- **Risk analysis**: In any financial institute there are many business risks involved like fraud, cyber attacks and loan defaulters. Big data analytics can be used to identify potential risks and their possible impacts which helps organizations in implementing counter measures in time.

12.9 Sport

Important applications of big data analytics in the sport industry include:

- **Player, team and fan management analysis**: Incorporating big data analytics in sport is the new trend. Most companies and franchisees are using big data analytics to get a competitive edge by analyzing various factors related to different teams, individual players and their fan bases.
- **Structuring player contracts**: Big data analytics is used by different sport franchises to deeply scrutinize the players based on different factors like recent performance, health issues and brand value for contracts.
- **Avoiding mishaps**: Big data analytics can be helpful in avoiding any mishap with players by analyzing their health parameters, environmental conditions, how much an individual is prone to a specific injury and other factors. Big data analytics can also contribute to avoiding mishaps in stadiums like fights between different fan groups.

12.10 Politics

Important applications of big data analytics in politics include:

- **Identifying ideological bias**: In recent years, many political parties have collaborated with agencies to identify the ideological biases in the public and decide their agendas for upcoming elections.
- **Trend analysis**: Social media is a very effective tool for trend analysis. Agencies use data from various sources like Twitter and Facebook to identify trends especially related to current affairs or controversial topics.
- **Evaluation of public reactions**: Big data analytics is very helpful in analyzing the sentiments of the public regarding political decisions or policies.

References

Amr, A., & Munshi, A. A. (2021). Big data platform for educational analytics. *IEEE Access, 9*, 52883–52890.

Bhat, S. A., & Huang, N. F. (2021). Big data and ai revolution in precision agriculture: Survey and challenges. *IEEE Access, 9*, 110209–110222.

Fan-Hsun Tseng, H.-H. C.-T. (2019). Applying big data for intelligent agriculture-based crop selection analysis. *IEEE Access, 7*, 116965–116974.

Guanlin Zhai, Y. Y. (2020). Multi-attention fusion modeling for sentiment analysis of educational big data. *Big Data Mining and Analytics, 3*(4),311–319.

Haili Wang, N. L. (2020). A personalized movie recommendation system based on LSTM-CNN. *2nd International Conference on Machine Learning, Big Data and Business Intelligence (MLBDBI)* (pp. 485–490).

Ijaz Ul Haq, K. M. (2019). DeepStar: Detecting starring characters in movies. *IEEE Access, 7*, 9265–9272.

Kenneth Li-Minn Ang, F. L. (2020). Big educational data & Analytics: Survey, architecture and challenges. *IEEE Access, 8*, 116392–116414.

N Pelchat, C. G. (2020). Neural network music genre classification. *Canadian Journal of Electrical and Computer Engineering, 43*(3), 170–173.

Ruomu Miao, W. Y. (2022). Research on collaborative recommendation algorithm based on film and television big data. *11th International Conference of Information and Communication Technology (ICTech)* (pp. 282–286).

Araújo, S. O., Peres, R. S., Barata, J., Lidon, F., & Ramalho, J. C. (2021). Characterising the agriculture 4.0 landscape—Emerging trends, challenges and opportunities. *Agronomy, 11*(4), 667.

Simin Yang, C. N. (2021). Examining emotion perception agreement in live music performance. *IEEE Transactions on Affective Computing, 14*(2), 1442–1460.

Singh, R. K., Berkvens, R., & Weyn, M. (2021). AgriFusion: An architecture for IoT and emerging technologies based on a precision agriculture survey. *9*(2), *IEEE Access*, 136253–136283.

Singh, P. K., & Hussain, M. S. (2018). Expert system for crop selection in agriculture: A critical review. *International Journal of Advanced Research in Computer Science, 9*, 143–146.

Stavros Ntalampiras, I. P. (2019). A statistical inference framework for understanding music-related brain activity. *IEEE Journal of Selected Topics in Signal Processing, 13*(2), 275–284.

Tianshu Li, Y. C. (2018). A novel word cloud graph system design for movie comments. *International Conference on Cloud Computing, Big Data and Blockchain (ICCBB)* (pp. 1–5).

Xiang Liu, M. S. (2020). Research on application of university student behavior model based on big data technology. *5th International Conference on Mechanical, Control and Computer Engineering (ICMCCE)*, 5th International conference, (pp. 1387–1390).

Zhaoya Chen, W. H. (2020). Application and development of big data in sustainable utilization of soil and land resources. *IEEE Access, 8*, 152751–152759.

(2022).Hu, Z., Liu, Y., Chen, G., & Liu, Y. Can machines generate personalized music? A hybrid favorite-aware method for user preference music transfer. *Transactions on Multimedia, 25*, 2296–2308.

Index

Access control 144
  algorithms 109
Accounting fraud 151
Accuracy 17
Apache Flume 78
Apache Spark 79
Architecture 109
Audio analytics 167
Autoencoders 115

BASE model 92
Bidirectional recurrent neural
          networks (BRNN) 114
Big data 3, 10, 13
  Bigtable 62
Blockchain 124
Block linking 126
Blocks 124

CAP Theorem 91
Column-oriented databases 86
  convolutional layer 111
Completeness 17
Consensus mechanism 126
Consistency 17
Consortium blockchain 128
Convolutional neural network 110
Credit card fraud 150

Data aggregation 144
Data integration 23, 35
Data lakes 96
Data management 61
DataNode 64
Data preprocessing 35
Data processing 61
Data protection 36
Data quality 17, 30, 35
Data quality management 32
    data governance 33
    data profiling 33
    data matching 33
Data source 12
Data storage 60
Data swamps 100
Data transformation 35
Data type 12
Data visualization 35
Data warehouse 11, 12 , 29
Deep belief networks (DBN) 116
Deep learning 108
Delta Lake 103
Descriptive 47
Descriptive analytics 167
Diagnostic 49
Diagnostic analytics 167
Document-oriented databases 87

Extraction 25

Feature engineering 108
Feature extraction 118
Financial markets fraud 151
Fraud 148
    fully connected layer 111

Google File System (GFS) 62
Gated recurrent units (GRUs) 113
Graph-based databases 88

Hadoop 59
Hadoop Distributed File System
    (HDFS) 62
Hash 124
HBase 65
HIVE 71
Hybrid blockchain 128

Image analytics 167
Immutability 132
Insurance fraud 150

Kohonen map 114

Lake house 101
Loading 25
Long short-term memory (LSTM)
    113

MapReduce 68
Mediation 26
    ontology 26
    databank 26
Merkle tree root 125
Money laundering 150

NameNode 63
Network analysis 168
    networks 110

Network intrusion 150
NoSQL 81

Oozie 77

Payload 126
Pervasive healthcare 141
    pooling layer 111
Predictive 50
    forecast 52
    classification 52
    time series 52
    clustering 52
Predictive analytics 167
Prescriptive analytics 167
Private blockchain 127
Prospective 52
Public blockchain 126

Query 12

Recurrent neural networks 113
Restricted Boltzmann machines
    (RBM) 116

Securities market 151
Self-organized map
    (SOM) 114
Semi-structured data 5
Sentiment analysis 168
Social media 161
Storage in cloud 30
Structure 124
Structured data 4
Supervised learning 110

Telecommunication fraud 151
Text analytics 167
Time series analysis 168
Timeliness 17
Topic analysis 168

Transfer learning 118
Transformation 25
Transient zone 97
Trusted zone 98
Types of big data analytics 47

Uniqueness 17
Unstructured data 4
Unsupervised learning 114

Validity 17

Value 10
Variety 9
Velocity 9
Video analytics 167
Volume 8

Warehousing 25

YARN 69

ZooKeeeper 75